A HANDBOOK OF THE
UNITED
NATIONS

BY JACK E. VINCENT, Ph.D.
Florida Atlantic University

Barron's Educational Series, Inc., Woodbury, New York

ACKNOWLEDGEMENTS

I wish to thank, first and foremost, my wife, Shirley for her long hours of helpful assistance, particularly in typing and proof-reading. The generous support of the Florida Atlantic University Political Science Department, headed by Dr. John DeGrove, and, in particular, the services of Myrtle Cassel are greatly appreciated.

PREFACE

What are the functions of the Economic and Social Council? What is the difference between a "call upon" measure and a "decision" by the Security Council? What is a "double veto," a "roll call vote," a "special session" of the General Assembly? What decisions and advisory opinions have been given by the International Court of Justice? Hundreds of questions such as these are clearly and concisely answered in this volume. Everyone is aware of the great importance of the United Nations in contemporary world affairs. Within this volume is found an accurate survey of the numerous structures and concepts which make up the United Nations system.

Designed for quick easy reference by having all entries arranged alphabetically, the volume can be used by almost anyone, from one with the most elementary background to the graduate student focusing his attention on the United Nations. In particular, it should be an invaluable aid to teachers and students of World History, American History, Contemporary History, American Problems, Civics, and Surveys of Social Science, at the high school level; and Modern Government, American Government, American Foreign Policy, Problems of Peace and Conflict, International Law, International Politics, International Relations, and International Organization. In addition, lay citizens with a special interest in the United Nations can quickly broaden their knowledge and perspective about the organization through a perusal of the volume.

Available also is a companion volume entitled, *A Handbook of International Relations: A Guide to Terms, Theory and Practice*. Written with the same design and purposes, it covers numerous structures, such as the Organization of American States and Arab League. It also covers the operating rules, such as those pertaining to prisoners of war, as well as theoretical conceptions, such as field theory and systems theory, which have pertinence to international relations and foreign affairs. Together the two volumes provide a wealth of concentrated information which could only be gained through a careful examination of hundreds of books and articles and perhaps not even then. Thumbing through either volume will convincingly reveal the breadth and scholarship of these much needed references.

INTRODUCTION

The United Nations came into formal existence on October 24, 1945. Its Charter was drafted by delegates of fifty nations which met in San Francisco from April 25–June 26, 1945. The General Assembly held its first session on January 10, 1946.

The United Nations is the second major collective security experiment in this century, the first being the League of Nations. Basically, the United Nations may be viewed as a resurrection of the League, but with certain modifications to fill the gaps and deficiencies of the League system.

First, states pledge, upon becoming members of the United Nations, that they will not use force or the threat of force against the territorial integrity and political independence of other states, except in their own self-defense. In short, the United Nations system seems to illegalize "a state of war" defined as a situation of equal co-belligerency. This stands in contrast to the legal situation in the League system where war was allowable under certain circumstances.

Second, under the United Nations system, states give the Security Council the right to make a determination as to whether the Charter has been violated and they pledge to support the decisions of the Security Council. In the League system, on the other hand, each state decided for itself whether the Covenant had been violated and whether sanctions should be applied, although the League Council could make recommendations in these respects.

Third, it was envisioned at San Francisco that the

United Nations would acquire a military force donated by member states, under the control of the Security Council, to be used in the maintenance of peace and security. In the League system, on the other hand, any collective enforcement action stayed in national hands.

Fourth, many of the procedures of the United Nations are more liberal, from a supranational point of view, than those of the League of Nations. In particular, the United Nations employs (basically) a majority voting system for both the Security Council and General Assembly. This stands in contrast to the unanimity system of the League Council and Assembly. Although the five permanent members of the Security Council do possess a veto over any Council decisions, in the League system, every state, that was not a party to a dispute, possessed such a privilege in Council and the Assembly.

Finally, the basic principles of the League collective security system are modified. In the League system it was assumed that all states would react against any aggressor while in the United Nations system special emphasis is put upon the responsibilities of the permanent members of the Security Council. Thus, the fundamental principle of the League may be characterized as "all against the few" while the UN principle might be characterized as "the big against the middle sized and small."

Although the United Nations can be seen, thus far, as more successful in accomplishing its objectives than the League, nevertheless, it is clear that the framers at San Francisco misjudged the readiness of states to accept the new system.

First, they misjudged the willingness of states to place permanent military contingents under the United Nations. As the system has worked out, the United Nations does not possess a much stronger collective security capability, defined as standing forces, than the League did.

Second, they misjudged the readiness of the permanent

members of the Security Council to cooperate with one another in respect to peace and security matters. As it turns out, the permanent members of the Security Council are frequently at loggerheads over, and frequently deeply involved in, the very crises that they were, presumably, to resolve.

Third, they misjudged the willingness of states generally to support the collective security principle. Thus, the United Nations has seen little more support of collective security actions than was the case in the League. The most important "test case" in this regard was the Korean conflict which saw a number of states ignoring the UN or actually aiding the side opposite to which the United Nations was committed.

In general, there has been a tendency for many states to return to the classical state behavior patterns evidenced in the League system and before it. That is, there is a tendency to create alliances, which make grave inroads into collective security pledges, in the sense that it is unlikely that military allies will act against one another, and to engage in unilateral action, that is, action basically outside of the United Nations framework in order to accomplish objectives. The US-British military actions during the Lebanon crisis (1958) and US military action in the Dominican Republic (1965) and Vietnam (1965–) seem to fall in this category. Also, unilateralism and self-help are evident in the French-British-Israel invasion of Egypt (1956), the USSR's action in Hungary (1956) and India's "conquest" of the enclaves of Goa, Diu and Damao (1961).

On the other hand, it cannot be said that the United Nations has been without effect upon the behavior of states since World War II. It seems fairly clear that it has had distinctly pacifying effects on a number of important crises; most notably, Korea, Suez, Congo, and Cyprus. Further, the United Nations has served as an important channel of communication between states and a funnel through which funds and technical assistance are given to the bulk of the under-developed countries of the world.

AD HOC COMMITTEE
OF EIGHTEEN

The *Ad Hoc* Committee of Eighteen was created by the General Assembly in 1958 to study the problems connected with the exploration of outer space. The Soviet Union and its allies, however, refused to cooperate with the Committee because of its composition. The Committee did direct itself to numerous technical problems, however, before it was expanded and re-named the Committee on the Peaceful Uses of Outer Space in 1959.

ATOMIC ENERGY
COMMISSION

The Atomic Energy Commission was created by the General Assembly, in January, 1946, to work out a plan for the control of atomic energy. During its life, the Commission reported to the Security Council and was composed of the members of the Security Council plus Canada. Although the General Assembly endorsed the Baruch Plan to guide the Commission in respect to the control of atomic energy, the USSR offered alternative plans. This lead to a deadlock in the Commission, by 1948. The principal points of disagreement included: (1) the question of the veto applying in Security Council decisions relating to the Commission's work, (2) the problem of the kind and extent of inspection and controls, and (3) the question of national vs. international ownership. In general, the Soviet Union opposed the supranational character of the "Western" proposals (i.e., the USSR wanted the veto, more limited inspection, and national ownership). AEC was disbanded in 1952, with the formation of the Disarmament Commission.

"BIG FIVE"

"Big Five" is the term used to describe the states which were considered most important at the end of World War II and which possess special privileges in the United Nations. These states are the United States, United Kingdom, France, China, and the Soviet Union. One of them, China, has relinquished her United Nation's position to Taiwan—in fact, although not in "theory." That is, at present, the United Nations only recognizes "one China," which is represented by delegates from Taiwan. The "big five," special, United Nations privileges consist of: (1) a permanent seat on and veto power in the Security Council; (2) a permanent seat on the Trusteeship Council; and (3) repeated election, through gentlemen's agreements, to the International Court of Justice, the Economic and Social Council, and to the Vice-Presidencies of the General Assembly. These latter positions (Vice-Presidencies), in turn, provide automatic presence on the General Committee.

"CALL UPON"
MEASURES

"Call upon" measures may either have the character of a recommendation or a decision, depending upon the provisions of the Charter relied upon. Because the General Assembly is limited to making recommendations, anytime states are "called upon" to do something by the General Assembly they are free, technically, to refuse compliance.

2

When the Security Council is operating under provisions other than those in Chapter VII its "call upon" measures seem to have the same weight as those of the General Assembly. However, when states are "called upon" in respect to provisional measures (Article 40), non-military, collective enforcement (Article 41), and collective military enforcement (Article 42, 43) the Security Council "request" is binding and has the same status as a rule of international law.

CAUCUSING GROUPS

A United Nations caucusing group is an organization of member states which meets with some degree of regularity for the purpose of discussing questions and issues connected with the United Nations. All of the caucusing groups, that is, the Soviet, Afro-Asian, Asian, African, Arab, Scandinavian, Benelux, European Community, Western European (and others), and Latin American groups, tend to have a geographic base. Not all the members of a particular geographic area, however, may be members of a group or even be viewed as desirable members. For example, the Union of South Africa is not a member of the African or Afro-Asian groups. Also, members from outside a geographic region may meet with a group on certain matters. For example, the United States and Japan meet with the Western European (and others) group on economic and legal matters. In this connection, Canada, Australia, and New Zealand are regular members of the Western European (and others) group. The Commonwealth group, without a geographic basis, at one time was considered a caucusing group, but is no longer considered so because of the infrequency and informality of its meetings.

Some caucusing groups are groups within larger groups. For example, all of the members of the Arab, African and

Asian groups are members of the Afro-Asian group. (Somewhat earlier, the situation was even more complicated when the Casablanca and Brazzaville groups were subdivisions of the African group and the Casablanca group cut into the membership of the Arab group). Also, the Scandinavian, European Community, and Benelux groups are subdivisions of the Western European (and others) group. Ignoring such subdivisions, however, four fairly distinct groups emerge, that is, the Soviet, Afro-Asian, Western European, and Latin American groups.

In general, the less economically developed a group's members are, the more supranational their views tend to be concerning caucusing group activity. Thus, members of less developed groups, such as the Arab and Afro-Asian groups, are more likely to see caucusing group activity having impact on their national governments, express a desire to make caucusing group decisions binding, and view caucusing group activity as helping the United Nations more than members of the more developed groups, such as the Western European (and others) and Soviet groups. Also, the meetings of the less developed groups tend to be more frequent and cover a greater range of issues than those of the developed groups.

Although caucusing groups do not make decisions that are binding upon their members, nevertheless the interaction which goes on between members during meetings helps shape their attitudes toward resolutions and elections. Also, it is not uncommon for a single member of a caucusing group to speak on behalf of the entire group, after a consensus has been reached.

CHAPTER VI

Chapter VI refers to Articles 33–38 in the United Nation's Charter relating to pacific settlement of disputes. These provisions pertain, basically, to international situations

and disputes which are serious enough to be "likely to endanger international peace and security." They are not so
dangerous, however, as to actually constitute a threat to the
peace, a breach of the peace, or an act of aggression (treated
in Chapter VII). Both the Security Council and the General
Assembly are treated in Chapter VI, in the sense that situations and disputes may be brought to their attention. Only
the Security Council is mentioned, however, in the detailed
procedural provisions of Chapter VI. Presumably, then, the
General Assembly is free from the various procedural restrictions put upon the Security Council, in respect to the treatment
of disputes and situations; although, the General Assembly
cannot make recommendations on disputes or situations being
considered by the Security Council unless the Security Council
so requests (Article 12 (1)). Because the matters treated in
Chapter VI are less serious than those covered in Chapter VII,
the Security Council and the General Assembly are limited by
Chapter VI to making recommendations. When the Security
Council applies Chapter VI, however, members of the Security
Council must "abstain" from voting (permanent members
lose their veto) if they are a party to a dispute. On the other
hand, any determination concerning whether to operate under
Chapter VI is subject to the veto.

CHAPTER VII

Chapter VII details Security Council responsibilities in
respect to the collective security functions of the United
Nations. Chapter VII applies when the Security Council determines that there is a "threat to the peace," a "breach of
the peace," or "acts of aggression" in the international community. Such a determination stands in contrast to that made
in connection with Chapter VI concerning disputes and situations "likely" to endanger international peace and security.
The Security Council is empowered under Chapter VII to

make recommendations; restore peace and security (Article 39); call upon disputants to comply with provisional measures (i.e., cease fire, Article 40) and/or make decisions in respect to non-military measures (i.e., severance of economic relations, Article 41) and/or military measures (Article 42). The failure of the Military Staff Committee to secure arrangements for armed forces contributions to be made to the Security Council, provided by Article 43, however, limits the Security Council, at present, to *deciding* upon non-military measures and *recommending* military measures. Although the General Assembly is not mentioned in Chapter VII, the Uniting for Peace Resolution seems to give the Assembly the same recommendation powers, instead of decision powers (qualified above), in respect to Articles 41 and 42.

CHARTER

The United Nations Charter is the legal document providing for the objectives, procedures, and organs, with their relationships and power, of the United Nations system. The Charter was unanimously adopted at the San Francisco Conference, attended by fifty states, held from April 25 to June 26, 1945. The Charter was subsequently ratified by the original members.

Important prior steps leading to the adoption of the Charter at San Francisco were: (1) the construction and failure of the League of Nations system; (2) the issuance, in August, 1941, of the "Atlantic Charter"; (3) the endorsement of the Atlantic Charter by twenty-six allied powers, in January, 1942, in their "Declaration by United Nations"; (4) a commitment by the United States, United Kingdom, USSR and China to construct a "general international organization . . . for the maintenance of international peace and security" in their "Moscow Declaration" of October, 1943;

(5) an agreement on the broad outlines of the United Nations by the United States, United Kingdom, USSR, and China at the Dumbarton Oaks Conference of August–October, 1944; and (6) an agreement on certain unsolved details, particularly the question of the "veto" power, by the United States, USSR, and the United Kingdom, at the Yalta Conference of February, 1945.

These steps show that the document was primarily the work of "great powers," and this fact is reflected in the powers and responsibilities of the members and the UN organs, particularly in respect to the predominance of the Security Council in peace and security matters and the permanent presence of the great powers on that organ. The influence of the smaller and medium powers was felt at San Francisco, however, especially on the matters of keeping the composition of the Security Council's agenda and the discussion of it "veto free" and the question of enlarging the scope, role, and status of the Economic and Social Council and the Trusteeship Council.

The purposes of the organization, as agreed upon at San Francisco, are as follows:

1. maintain international peace and security, and, to that end: to take effective collective measures for the prevention and removal of threats to the peace, and for the suppression of acts of aggression or other breaches of the peace, and to bring about by peaceful means, and in conformity with the principles of justice and international law, adjustment or settlement of international disputes or situations which might lead to a breach of the peace;

2. to develop friendly relations among nations based on respect for the principle of equal rights and self-determination of peoples, and to take other appropriate measures to strengthen universal peace;

3. to achieve international cooperation in solving international problems of an economic, social, cultural, or humanitarian character, and in promoting and encouraging respect for human rights and for fundamental freedoms

7

for all without distinction as to race, sex, language, or religion; and

4. to be a center for harmonizing the actions of nations in the attainment of these common ends. (Charter, Article 1)

In connection with these purposes, members pledge, among other things, to: (1) respect the "sovereign equality" of other members; (2) settle their international disputes by "peaceful means" so that "international peace and security, and justice, are not endangered"; (3) refrain from the "threat or the use of force against the territorial integrity or political independence of any state, or in any other manner inconsistent with the Purposes of the United Nations"; (4) give the United Nations "assistance" in action it undertakes in accordance with the Charter and "refrain from giving assistance to any state against which the United Nations is taking preventive or enforcement action." (Article 2)

Other articles treat: Membership; major organs; pacific settlement of disputes; actions with respect to threats and breaches of the peace and acts of aggression; regional arrangements; international, economic, and social cooperation; non-self-governing territories; the trusteeship system; miscellaneous provisions; transitional security arrangements; amendments; and ratification. (45, 132, 139, 257)

CHARTER

Amendments

Amendments to the Charter come into force after having been voted for adoption by two-thirds of the members of the General Assembly and ratification by two-thirds of the member states including all of the permanent members of the Security Council. Thus, each permanent member of the Security Council possesses a veto over possible amendments. Amendments are binding on all member states, whether ratified by them or not. However, unfavorable amendments, as viewed at the San Francisco Conference, may be grounds for withdrawal from the organization. Since the tenth annual session, a conference to review the Charter can be called by a majority vote of the General Assembly and a procedural vote of the Security Council (no veto). Prior to the tenth session, such a conference required a two-thirds vote in the General Assembly and a procedural vote in the Security Council. If a conference is held, proposed amendments will come into force when ratified by two-thirds of the Members including all of the permanent members of the Security Council. Amendments proposed in 1963 by the General Assembly, to increase the membership of the Security Council and Economic and Social Council, came into legal effect, after sufficient ratifications, on August 31, 1965.

CHARTER

Legal Status

Article 103 establishes the pre-eminence of the Charter over any other international obligation. It stipulates "in the event of a conflict between the obligations of the Members of the United Nations and of the present Charter and their obligations under any other international agreement, their obligations under the Charter shall prevail." For example, if a state were to enter into agreement so that it was obligated not to view the Security Council's decisions under Article 41 as binding, such an obligation, itself, would not be binding in the legal sense, because of Article 103. Thus, although the Charter is a treaty, it is a treaty of a special kind which, short of amendment to change this provision, has priority over future treaties in a way not unlike a constitution's priority over ordinary law. In the case of ordinary treaties, they can simply be overturned by future treaties as municipal, ordinary laws can be overturned by new laws.

9

CHILDREN'S FUND
UNICEF

The United Nations International Children's Emergency Fund was created by the General Assembly, in December, 1946, to provide emergency relief for children because of conditions resulting from World War II. This mission, continued until 1950, resulted in a flow of food, medical supplies, and clothing to needy children, when, with post-war reconstruction basically accomplished, the General Assembly broadened the functions of UNICEF and focused its activities upon the children of underdeveloped areas. In 1953, the organization's name was changed to the United Nations Children's Fund and established on a permanent basis, although the UNICEF abbreviation remained the same. Since that time, the Fund has focused on stimulating projects in health, welfare, disease, nutrition, education, and vocational training. UNICEF partially finances governmental projects in recipient states and coordinates projects with work of other agencies such as the World Health Organization. The principal organs of UNICEF are the Executive Board and the Executive-Director (with his staff). Although the structure and functions of UNICEF are similar to those of specialized agencies, technically, UNICEF remains a subsidiary organ of the General Assembly, reporting to the Economic and Social Council (ECOSOC). The Central Headquarters are located in New York with regional and field offices scattered throughout the world.

UNICEF

Executive Board

The Executive Board consists of thirty members elected by the Economic and Social Council from members of the specialized agencies and the United Nations. Its function is to establish policy in respect to UNICEF activities and to allocate fund monies for those projects the Board has decided to support.

Executive Director

The Executive Director is appointed by the Secretary-General of the United Nations after consultation with the Executive Board. The Executive Director administers the Fund and directs the UNICEF staff according to the policies established by the Executive Board. The Director reports annually to ECOSOC and that organ takes note of the report and may use the occasion to make recommendations concerning UNICEF activities.

Financing

Unlike a specialized agency which typically receives its income from member states according to a scale of contributions relating to a budget, UNICEF operates completely through voluntary contributions and the sale of greeting cards. Contributions are received from governments, private organizations, and private persons. The number of governments contributing has constantly increased so that almost every government makes some contribution. Government contributions constitute the bulk of UNICEF's income and an operating fund, presently set at fifty million dollars by the Executive Board, allows UNICEF, depending upon Board policy, to spend more than it receives in any one year.

COMMISSION FOR
CONVENTIONAL ARMAMENTS

The Commission for Conventional Armaments was created by the Security Council, after a General Assembly resolution of December, 1946, which stressed the international need for the regulation and reduction of national armed forces. The Commission's work was to focus on conventional armaments and, therefore, was to supplement but not overlap the work of the Atomic Energy Commission (AEC). The Commission was composed of the members of the Security Council, both permanent and non-permanent, and reported to the Security Council. During Commission meetings, disagreements between the Communist and other members centered on: (1) the question of including weapons of mass destruction in the Commission's work (Communists favored); (2) making the acceptance of disarmament plans contingent upon the establishment of military forces under the Security Council, the control of atomic energy, and the conclusion of peace treaties with Japan and Germany (Communists basically opposed preconditions); and (3) the nature and function of international control and supervision (Communists basically opposed extensive controls). Commission proposals, in the form of a report approved by a Commission, non-communist majority, received a USSR veto in the Security Council in 1949. Effective work by the Commission ended in April, 1950, when the USSR withdrew, protesting the representation on the Commission of the Republic of China instead of Communist China. The Commission was disbanded in January, 1952, with the creation of the Disarmament Commission.

COMMITTEE ON THE PEACEFUL USES OF OUTER SPACE

The Committee on the Peaceful Uses of Outer Space was formed by the General Assembly in 1959 by expanding the *Ad Hoc* Committee of Eighteen. Since then disputes between East and West, similar to those which have existed in the Disarmament Commission and the Eighteen-Nation Disarmament Commission, have hampered the Committee's work. In 1965, however, the Committee was able to issue a Declaration, approved by the General Assembly, which stressed the: (1) freedom of states to explore outer space; (2) extension of international law to outer space; (3) need for cooperation between states engaging in exploration of the same areas; (4) application of each state's jurisdiction to its own space vehicles; and (5) the need for all states to cooperate and give assistance to states engaged in space exploration, particularly in cases of emergency landings and similar situations. These concepts have been incorporated into the "Treaty in the Principles of the Activity of States in the Exploration and Use of Outer Space, including the Moon and Other Celestial Bodies."

CONNALLY RESOLUTION

The Connally Resolution of November 5, 1943, initiated by Senator Tom Connally of Texas, expressed the commitment of the Senate of the United States to the United Nations by recognizing "the necessity of there being established at the earliest practical date a general international organization, based on the principle of the sovereign equality of all peace-loving states, and open to the membership of all such states, large and small, for the maintenance of international peace and security" (260, p. 14). The Connally Resolution (passed eighty-five to five), although not binding upon individual senators in respect to their vote to commit the United States to the United Nations Charter, nevertheless, clearly revealed the Senate support for the United Nations in contrast to the earlier rejection by the Senate of the League of Nations.

DECISIONS

A decision, in contrast to a recommendation, is considered binding upon states and, therefore, is similar to a rule of international law. In the United Nations system only the International Court of Justice and the Security Council are empowered to make decisions. Whenever the Court has jurisdiction and decides a case or provisional measures a state is considered to have committed a delict if it refuses compliance. The Security Council makes decisions binding on states only when it operates under Article 41, which applies to non-forceful collective security measures, and Article 42, pertaining to forceful collective security measures. The latter provisions, however, are contingent upon the establishment of special agreements between force contributing states and the Security Council. Because these agreements have never come into effect, the Security Council is limited to making decisions in respect to Article 41 but only recommendations in respect to Article 42. Although the term "decide" is used elsewhere in the Charter it does not refer, in these cases, to "decisions" binding upon states (i.e., the Security Council may "decide" to operate under Article 36, allowing recommendations as to the mode of pacific settlement, if parties to a dispute refer a dispute to the Security Council).

CONVENTION ON THE PRIVILEGES AND IMMUNITIES OF THE UNITED NATIONS

The Convention on The Privileges and Immunities of the United Nations was approved by the General Assembly in 1947. The Assembly encouraged accession by all member states. Among its provisions are ones providing for: (1) freedom from taxation for the United Nations and the salaries of United Nations officials, including tax-free operations of

United Nations organs (i.e., UNICEF); (2) travel rights by UN officials into and out of member states which adhere to the Convention (through the use of a *laizze passer* issued by the United Nations); (3) the right of the United Nations to contract and initiate legal proceedings; (4) immunity from legal proceedings against the property and assets of the United Nations; (5) the inviolability of United Nations property and assets from search, requisition, confiscation, and expropriation; (6) the right of the United Nations to hold and deal with assets and property; (7) freedom from interference and censorship regarding United Nations publications and communications; and (8) privileges and immunities for United Nations diplomats and members of the Secretariat. The bulk of the member states (not including the United States) have adhered to the Convention. The arrangements between the United States and the United Nations are specified in a Headquarters Agreement. (92)

DECLARATION ON THE GRANTING OF INDEPENDENCE TO COLONIAL COUNTRIES AND PEOPLES

The Declaration on the Granting of Independence to Colonial Countries and Peoples was adopted by the General Assembly on December 14, 1960. Although no state voted against the Declaration, nine states abstained from voting— the United States, United Kingdom, Australia, Belgium, Dominican Republic, France, Portugal, Spain, and South Africa. The Declaration: (1) views the subjugation of peoples by alien powers as contrary to the United Nations Charter; (2) gives all people the right of self-determination in respect to their political status and their economic, social, and cultural development; (3) calls for an end to any kind of armed action or repressive measures to prevent dependent people from gaining their independence; (4) calls for the transference of power without condition to peoples wishing independence; (5) views an effort to disrupt the national unity or territorial integrity of a country as contrary to the Charter of the United Nations; and (6) calls upon states to observe the UN Charter, the Universal Declaration of Human Rights, and the Declaration on the Granting of Independence to Colonial Countries and Peoples.

The June, 1967, Annual Report of the Secretary-General showed the General Assembly's concern with and discussion of the following territories in connection with the implementation of the Declaration: Southern Rhodesia, South West Africa, Portuguese territories, Aden, Basutoland, Bechuanaland, Swaziland, French Somaliland, Equatorial Guinea, Ifni and Spanish Sahara, Gibralter, Fiji, Mauritius, Falkland Islands, American Samoa, Antigua, Bahamas, Bermuda, British Virgin Islands, Cayman Islands, Cocos Islands, Dominica, Gilbert and Ellice Islands, Grenada, Guam, Montserrat, New Hebrides, Niue, Pitcairn, St. Helena, St. Kitts-Nevis-Anguilla, St. Lucia, St. Vincent, Seychelles, Solomon Islands, Tokelau Islands, Turks and Caicos Islands, Virgin Islands, and Oman.

DECLARATION REGARDING NON-SELF-GOVERNING TERRITORIES

States responsible for non-self-governing territories assume certain responsibilities for them by virtue of being members of the United Nations. Such states promise, under Article 73, to:

> promote . . . the well-being of the inhabitants . . . to ensure . . . political, economic, social and educational advancement . . . [and] . . . to transmit regularly to the Secretary General . . . subject to such limitation as security and constitutional considerations may require, statis-

tical and other information . . . relating to economic, social and educational conditions in the territories.

Also, responsible states promise that their policy toward the territories should take "due account . . . of the interests and well-being of the rest of the world, in social, economic, and commercial matters" (Article 74). The organs primarily concerned with the implementation of these provisions are the Special Committee and the Trusteeship Committee (Fourth) of the General Assembly. UN consideration of non-self-governing matters revolves, for the most part, around information gathered from questionnaires completed by the responsible states. Unlike the questionnaire used by the Trusteeship Council, however, the completion of the "political section" is optional. That is, only the non-political "general information", "economic", "social", and "educational" sections, because of the provisions of Article 73, are "required." In the past, considerable tension and debate have developed over the United Nations efforts to implement these articles. Several "colonial" powers have held that the above provisions are only moral obligations, the application of which is to be determined solely by the responsible states while many "non-colonial" states have viewed the provisions as binding, the interpretation of which should be determined by the United Nations.

UNITED NATIONS
DEVELOPMENT PROGRAMME

The United Nations Development Programme has brought together into one program, effective January 1, 1966, the Expanded Programs of Technical Assistance and the Special Fund. During 1965, before their merger, the two programs spent approximately $115,000,000 in support of more than 3,000 projects, involving some 150 states and territories.

On January 19, 1967, the Governing Council of UNDP approved seventy-one development projects, entailing costs of more than $186,000,000 and involving sixty-nine states and territories. UNDP will provide $78,800,000 of the total and the recipients $107,300,000. Twenty-six of the recipients are located in Africa and will receive $28,700,000; sixteen are located in the Americas and will receive $20,300,-000; sixteen are located in Asia and the Far East and will receive $16,200,000; six are located in Europe and will receive $7,300,000; and six are located in the Middle East and will receive $6,400,000. This decision raised the total number of Governing Council approved projects to 727, involving a total project value of about $1,800,000,000.

Pledges for the 1967 operations amount to $157,320,-684 pledged by 101 governments by November 2, 1966. Pledges are expected to rise to $167,400,000 but still fall short of the target figure of $200,000,000 set by the Secretary-General. The Special Fund component should reach approximately $106,600,000 and the Technical Assistance component about $60,800,000. The US 1967 pledge is $70,000,000 but is contingent upon the proviso that this amount does not exceed forty per cent of the total contributions of all states to the two components. In 1966, 112 governments pledged $154,900,000 of which $98,600,000 was for the Special Fund and $56,300,000 for Technical Assistance.

DISARMAMENT COMMISSION

The General Assembly created the Disarmament Commission in January, 1952, after an address by President Truman to the Assembly, in 1950, on the desirability of merging the work of the Commission for Conventional Armaments and the Atomic Energy Commission. The new Commission, therefore, considers all phases of disarmament, in contrast to the previous division of labor between the "atomic" and "conventional" commissions.

The members of the Disarmament Commission, initially, were members of the Security Council plus Canada. It was charged with formulating plans that would incorporate an international control organ, verification and disclosure schemes, and a system of safeguards.

As in the case of the two previous Commissions, however, disagreements between East and West continued upon basically the same lines. That is, the West tended to stress the need for "inspection" and "control" while the USSR and its allies have stressed the need to illegalize nuclear weapons and dismantle foreign bases.

After initial focus upon a "general plan" of disarmament and possible force level "freezes" in the arms race, discussions have tended to center more and more upon "disclosure" and possible warning systems against surprise attack. Discussions have included the possibility of creating aerial inspection zones within the USSR, Europe, and the United States.

In 1957, the General Assembly decided to enlarge the Disarmament Commission by adding fourteen members, but, at this time, the Soviet Union began to agitate for the inclusion of all United Nations members. Finally, in 1958, the Commission was expanded to include all UN members, but, since that time, it has been eclipsed by other disarmament developments, both inside and outside the United Nations. Of particular importance, in this respect, was the formation by the General Assembly, in 1959, of a new Ten-Nation Committee on Disarmament.

DUMBARTON OAKS CONFERENCE

The Dumbarton Oaks Conference (August 21–October 7, 1944) consisted of meetings among the United States,

USSR, Great Britain, and China to establish agreement upon and the framework for the establishment of the United Nations. China and the USSR did not interact in the meetings and China met with the United States and Great Britain after (during September 29–October 7) they had met with the USSR. Basically, China simply endorsed the work of the other parties. The meeting arrangements were the result of the fact that the USSR was a "neutral" in respect to the Chinese–Japanese War and felt that interaction with China might affect her status. The meetings led to the issuance of the Dumbarton Oaks Proposals which became the core agenda for the San Francisco Conference. The Proposals established that the United Nations would have primary responsibility in respect to maintaining international peace and security and they also outlined the major functions and relationships of the principal organs (with the exception of the Trusteeship Council). The Proposals, however, did not clarify the voting system of the Security Council and certain other important matters which were taken up later at the Yalta Conference.

ECONOMIC AND SOCIAL COUNCIL (ECOSOC)

The Economic and Social Council is designated as a principal organ of the United Nations (Article 7) and is responsible for promoting the objectives, set forth in Chapter IX of the Charter, concerning international economic and social cooperation. This includes concern with the promotion of "higher standards of living, full employment, and conditions of economic and social progress and development; solutions of international economic, social, health, and related problems; international cultural and educational cooperation; and universal respect for and observance of human rights and fundamental freedoms for all without distinction as to race, sex, language, or religion." In connection with these responsibilities, the Economic and Social Council may make and initiate studies and make recommendations to the General Assembly, member states, or the specialized agencies. Within its sphere of competence, the Council may draft international conventions for submission to the General Assembly, call for international conferences, and perform special services at the request of member states.

Specialized agencies which also operate in the economic, social, cultural, educational, health, and related fields are coordinated by the Economic and Social Council in terms of agreements reached between these agencies and the Council.

In all of its work, the Council operates "under the authority of the General Assembly." Thus, such matters as the nature of agreements with the specialized agencies, the calling of international conferences, and the submission of draft resolutions to member states must win the approval of the General Assembly. In fact, two of the General Assembly's main committees—the Economic and Financial and the Social, Humanitarian, and Cultural—devote a considerable portion of their attention to the Economic and Social Council's work.

The Council, because of its variegated objectives and the wide-flung nature of the numerous organs reporting to it and working with it, has been constantly plagued with the problem of coordination and integration of the activities for which it is responsible. (18, 91, 202)

ECONOMIC AND SOCIAL COUNCIL

"Category A"

"Category A" refers to non-governmental organizations (NGO's) which have been given this status because of the high degree of relationship between their work and that of the Council. Organizations so classified are the International Chamber of Commerce, International Confederation of Free Trade Unions, International Co-operative Alliance, International Federation of Agricultural Producers, International Federation of Christian Trade Unions, International Organization of Employers, Inter-Parliamentary Union, World Federation of Trade Unions, World Federation of United Nations Associations, and World Veterans Federation. The "rights" of these organizations are greater than those in "Category B." They include the right to: (1) propose items for the provisional agenda of the Council and its commissions (may not be accepted), (2) submit written statements (2000 words or less) to the Council and its commissions, (3) observe public meetings, (4) consult with standing committees of the Council upon request, and (5) appear before the Council upon recommendation of a standing committee. Organizations are reviewed annually in respect to their status.

"Category B"

"Category B" refers to non-governmental organizations (NGO's) given this status because they have interest in certain aspects of the Council's work. Approximately 120 organizations, including various business, professional, economic, social, and religious groups, hold the "B" rating and they possess fewer "rights" than those organizations in "Category A". Category B organizations have the right to: (1) submit written statements to the Council (500 words) and commissions (2000 words), (2) observe public meetings, and (3) consult with Council committees upon request. NGO's are reviewed annually in respect to their status.

Commission on Narcotic Drugs

The Commission on Narcotic Drugs is a functional commission, consisting of representatives appointed by the

Council from twenty-four states which are important drug producers or which have a serious problem of illicit drug traffic. The Commission: (1) advises the Council on conventions relating to drug control, (2) investigates and advises on United Nations related drug control machinery, (3) reviews and advises on individual countries' control measures, (4) investigates "new" drugs as to their danger and use and makes recommendations, and (5) can invite other organs, such as the World Health Organization, to undertake studies. The Commission reports to the Council and its recommendations may form the basis of Council and/or General Assembly recommendations. In general, the Commission forms the central organ of the drug control system and carries on the work of the League of Nations' Advisory Committee on Traffic in Opium and other Dangerous Drugs.

Committee on Non-Governmental Organizations

The Committee on Non-Governmental Organizations, consisting of seven members elected by the Council from Council members each year with the Council's President serving *ex officio,* screens non-governmental organizations requesting consultative status and makes recommendations to the Council concerning their status. It also considers, with the power of rejection, provisional agenda items proposed by organizations in "Category A."

Drug Supervisory Body

The Drug Supervisory Body was created, in 1931, by the Convention for Limiting the Manufacturing and Regulating the Distribution of Drugs. Its functions under the League System continued under the United Nations. Four independent experts, two appointed by the World Health Organization, one by the Permanent Central Opium Board, and one by the Commission of Narcotic Drugs, reviewed drug needs estimated by states and had the power to request revisions and explanations of estimates. States were limited in respect to their import and manufacture of drugs to limits based upon their estimates. The Supervisory Body reported to the Council and issued a publication entitled *Estimated World Requirements of Narcotic Drugs.* The Supervisory Body supplemented the work of the Permanent Central Opium Board and the Commission on Narcotic Drugs. After the Single Convention on Narcotic Drugs came into force, on December 13, 1964, the functions of the Drug Supervisory Commission were combined with those of the Central Opium Board to form a single agency, incorporating the central features of both. The new organ is composed of eleven experts and is called the International Narcotic Control Board.

ECONOMIC AND SOCIAL COUNCIL

Economic Commission for Africa (ECA)

The Economic Commission for Africa was created, on April 29, 1958, as a regional, economic commission under the Council. The Commission originally included all of the United Nations members of Africa (as well as France, Spain, Portugal, and the United Kingdom as especially interested states). Since 1963, however, South Africa has been suspended and Portugal excluded from the Commission. The headquarters and Secretariat are located in Addis Ababa, Ethiopia, where the annual sessions are held. The Commission gathers information on and fosters state cooperation in respect to matters such as agriculture, population growth, trade conservation, transport, power, resources, money, and education. For example, ECA helped organize and sponsor the Conference of African States on the Development of Education (1961). The Commission reports to the Council and publishes the *Economic Bulletin for Africa.*

24

Economic Commission for Asia and the Far East (ECAFE)

The Economic Commission for Asia and the Far East was created, on March 28, 1947, as a regional, economic commission under the Council. The Commission includes all of the United Nations members in the Asian and Far Eastern area (Iran eastward). Also included are France, Netherlands, USSR, United Kingdom, and the United States as non-Asian interested states, and South Korea and South Viet-Nam as non-United Nations Asian states. The headquarters and Secretariat are located in Bangkok, Thailand; although, the place of the annual sessions rotates among the regional member states. Through committees and bureaus, the Commission acquires information on and facilitates state cooperation in respect to transportation, communications, industrialization, exploitation of minerals, trade, flood control, and related matters in the Asian and Far Eastern area. The Commission reports to the Council and publishes *The Economic Survey of Asia and the Far East* (annual), the *Economic Bulletin of Asia and the Far East* (quarterly), and more specialized materials such as the *Mineral Resources Development Series*. Although Communist China is not a member of the Commission, data on China, where possible, is included in the surveys.

Economic Commission for Europe (ECE)

The Economic Commission for Europe was created, on March 28, 1947, as a regional, economic commission under the Council. All United Nations members in the European area are members of the Commission, including the USSR, Byelorussia, Ukraine, and the United Kingdom as well as West Germany as a full member, although not a United

Nations member, and the United States as a non-European, interested state. Switzerland holds a consultative status in respect to the Commission and its subsidiary organs, while Eastern Germany consults with the subsidiary organs. Those invited to participate on a consultative basis are not allowed to vote. The headquarters and permanent Secretariat are located in Geneva, where the annual meetings are held. Much of the work of the Commission is facilitated by committees that focus upon particular problems, such as agriculture, electrical power, transportation, housing, trade, timber and steel and examine such problems as supply, demand, quality cycles, trends and stabilization. Neither the Commission or its committees possess any decision making power, but their recommendations may lead to treaties. The Commission reports to the Council and publishes *The Economic Survey of Europe* (annual) and *Economic Bulletin for Europe* (quarterly) as well as specialized bulletins dealing with electrical, housing, and agricultural statistics.

ECONOMIC AND SOCIAL COUNCIL

Economic Commission for Latin America (ECLA)

The Economic Commission for Latin America was created, on February 25, 1948, as a regional, economic commission under the Council. The Commission includes all of the United Nations members in the Latin American area and Canada, France, Netherlands, United Kingdom, and the United States as especially interested states. The headquarters and Secretariat are located in Santiago, Chile, although the place of Commission sessions rotates among member states. The Commission, through various subgroups, makes studies and facilitates cooperation in respect to matters such as population, growth, trade, industry, labor, government efficiency, and economic integration. ECLA, for example, was actively involved in the creation of the Latin American Free Trade Area. The Commission reports to the Council and is responsible for *The Economic Survey of Latin America* (annual), the *Economic Bulletin for Latin America* (semi-annual), and other technical publications.

Functional Commissions

Functional Commissions are created to aid the Council and are authorized by Article 68 of the Charter. They focus on particular problems without geographic boundaries, in contrast to the Regional Economic Commissions. With the exception of the Commission on Narcotic Drugs (composed of important drug manufacturing states and ones with serious illegal drug traffic) the member states of the Commissions are elected by the Council to achieve geographic balance. Some Commissions, such as Statistical, International Commodity, and Population, focus upon technical data acquisition and analysis. Others, such as the Social Commission, Commission on Human Rights, and Commission on the Status of Women, combine data collection functions with recommendations as to policy. The Narcotics Commission, in addition to these functions, possesses a limited supervisory power based on conventions. The Commissions operate in a manner similar to the Council with a chairman, vice-chairman, and majority vote rule. Some meet annually and others every two years. Much important data published by the United Nations is the result of the work of the Commissions.

Invited Members

The Economic and Social Council may, if it deems it desirable because the matter under discussion is of particular concern to a member of the United Nations, invite that member without a vote to participate in the Council discussions (Charter, Article 69).

Membership

Members of the Economic and Social Council are elected by the General Assembly (two-thirds majority) for three-year, staggered terms with eligibility for reelection (Article 61). Prior to an amendment to the Charter, effective for the actual membership on January 1, 1966, the Council had eighteen members. Since then, the membership has been twenty-seven. The Council may invite members of the United Nations and arrange for representatives of specialized agencies to participate without vote in Council deliberations (Articles 69, 70). The "big five" with the exception of China have always been elected by the Assembly to the Council, although the UN Charter does not require it.

Nongovernmental Organizations

Nongovernmental Organizations (NGO's) are private groups, such as the International Chamber of Commerce or the World Federation of Trade Unions, which, according to Article 71 of the Charter, may enter into consultation with the Economic and Social Council, through arrangements agreed to by the Council. The Council recognizes two types of continuing consultative status, "Category A" and "Category B," for certain organizations. Other organizations, more tangential to the Council's work, are listed on a "register" and may be occasionally consulted. Such arrangements reflect the recognition of the importance of private efforts at international cooperation and the need to coordinate such work with the United Nations.

Permanent Central Opium Board

The Permanent Central Opium Board was created by the International Opium Convention of 1925. Its purpose and functions under the League of Nations continued under the United Nations. Eight independent experts were appointed, as such, for five-year terms by the Council to form the Board which had the primary duty of scrutinizing the reports of states required under the Convention as to the production, consumption, import, and export of narcotic drugs. State violations of drug conventions could have led, under the Convention, to consultation, inquiry (with permission), embargo on drugs, and, of course, publicity by the Board. The Board met twice a year and reported to the Council. *The Annual Summary of Laws and Regulations Relating to the Control of Narcotic Drugs, Annual Summary of Annual Reports of Governments, Summaries of Illicit Transactions and Seizures,* and the *Bulletin on Narcotics* are publications which related to the Board's work. After the Single Convention on Narcotic Drugs came into force, on December 13, 1964, the functions of the Central Opium Board were combined with those of the Drug Supervisory Commission to form a single agency, incorporating the central features of both. The new organ is composed of eleven experts and is called the International Narcotic Control Board.

Regional Economic Commissions

The Economic and Social Council, as authorized by Article 68 of the UN Charter, has established four regional economic commissions—the Economic Commission for Europe (ECE), the Economic Commission for Asia and the Far East (ECAFE), Economic Commission for Latin America (ECLA), and the Economic Commission for Africa (ECA).

The commissions include the members of the United Nations located in the region concerned and, possibly, certain non-United Nations members in the region, as well as non-regional members who have a special concern in the region. The commissions strive for regional, economic development through data collection and exchange of information and also initiate and coordinate projects. Commission functions are facilitated through the creation of various committees, sub-committees, and subsidiary organs. Each full commission meets regularly, reports to the Economic and Social Council, has a budget (part of the United Nations regular budget) and a permanent Secretariat. Valuable economic survey data and economic bulletins are published by the commissions.

ECONOMIC AND SOCIAL COUNCIL

Sessions

The Council normally holds both spring and summer sessions of approximately four to six weeks each year. The second session is reconvened after the General Assembly's session to consider the Assembly's resolutions relative to the Council's work and to plan for new sessions. Special sessions are held upon the call of the Security Council, General Assembly, or a majority of the members of the Council. Members of the United Nations and specialized agencies may request special sessions which will be held if the President and Vice-Presidents of the Council agree or a majority of Council members concur. Also, the President may call meetings if the Vice-Presidents agree.

ECONOMIC AND SOCIAL COUNCIL

"Special Bodies"

"Special Bodies" refers to certain Council-related organs that do not fit into the category of specialized agencies, functional commissions, or regional economic commissions, such as the United Nations Children's Fund and International Narcotics Board.

Technical Assistant Board (TAB)

The Technical Assistant Board, created in 1950, consisted of an executive chairman, appointed by the Secretary-General, and the heads of all specialized agencies participating in the United Nations Expanded Program of Technical Assistance. This included agencies such as the International Labor Organization, World Health Organization, World Meteorological Organization, and the United Nations Educational, Scientific, and Cultural Organization. TAB maintained offices and representatives in the many countries receiving United Nations aid, which assisted receiving governments in drawing up developmental plans and helped coordinate the work of the various agencies giving aid. National requests for aid were consolidated and related to existing funds by TAB which then submitted a general aid program to the Technical Assistance Committee. In 1964, ECOSOC recommended the consolidation of the Expanded Program of Technical Assistance with the Special Fund. The General Assembly, following the recommendations, created the United Nations Development Programme, which went into effect January 1, 1966. Under the new program the functions of TAB are absorbed by an Inter-Agency Consultative Board, consisting of participating agency executive heads and chaired by the Administrator or Co-Administrator of the Development Programme.

Technical Assistance Committee (TAC)

For years, the Technical Assistance Committee was a major organ in the Expanded Program of Technical Assistance. It was composed of thirty representatives, eighteen of which come from ECOSOC member states. The rest were elected by ECOSOC. It reported to ECOSOC on the coordination, effectiveness, and activities of the Expanded Program and authorized the allocation of funds to participating agencies. It was supplanted, in 1966, by the Governing Council, created by the United Nations Development Programme.

ECONOMIC AND SOCIAL COUNCIL

Voting

Each member of the Economic and Social Council has one vote and decisions are made by a simple majority of those present and voting (Article 67). Although, with the exception of China, the permanent members of the Security Council have always been elected to the Council, they possess no special privileges.

EDUCATIONAL, SCIENTIFIC AND CULTURAL ORGANIZATION (UNESCO)

United Nations Educational, Scientific and Cultural Organization (UNESCO) came into existence November 4, 1946, after twenty states had ratified its constitution, which had been adopted by a conference held in London in November, 1945, attended by forty-four states. UNESCO entered into a relationship with the United Nations in December, 1946, as a specialized agency, reporting to the Economic and Social Council. UNESCO's basic purposes are to contribute to peace and security by fostering cooperation in the educational, scientific, and cultural fields and to promote respect for justice, the rules of law, and fundamental rights and freedoms irrespective of race, sex, language, or religious differences. In this connection it functions to promote: exchanges of persons, artifacts, and publications; the development of educational facilities; and the preservation of books, art works, and cultural artifacts. UNESCO has the right to recommend conventions to states, engage in research, and participate in various regional and world development programs, i.e., currently one to make free, primary education available to children in Latin America. In such activities it renders a wide variety of informational and technical services. Thus, UNESCO frequently provides facts that are necessary to get a perspective on the basic world problems. Recently, for example, UNESCO estimated that between forty-three and forty-five percent of the world's adults are illiterate and that more than half of the children, between the ages of five to nineteen, in a majority of the countries of the world do not attend school.

The basic organs of UNESCO are the General Conference, the Executive Board, and the Director-General (Secretariat).

UNESCO produces numerous and diverse publications—such as *Bibliographical Services Throughout the World; Catalogs of Color Reproductions; Study Abroad; Vacations Abroad; The Race Question and Modern Science;* and *The History of Mankind, Cultural and Scientific Development.*

UNESCO's central headquarters are in Paris and it has several regional offices.

UNESCO

Director-General

The Director-General is the chief executive officer and is responsible for UNESCO's program and Secretariat staff of about 3,000 persons. He is nominated by the Executive Board and appointed for a six-year term by the General Conference. Under the supervision of the Executive Board he appoints and dismisses members of the staff and is responsible for budget estimates and the UNESCO work program.

Executive Board

The Executive Board consists of thirty individuals elected for four-year terms by the General Conference, with due regard for geographic, cultural diversity, and merit factors. The Board has supervisory responsibility for the UNESCO program, reviews the work program of the Director General, and makes recommendations to the General Conference. The Board normally meets twice a year.

Financing

After a two-year budget has been approved by the General Conference member states are assessed, as in the case of the United Nations, using a scale of contributions based upon ability to pay. The United States' share is approximately thirty percent; the USSR, fifteen percent; and so forth. In addition, UNESCO receives United Nations monies to cover the cost of its role in the United Nations Development Programme. Expenditures have constantly moved upward to the present level of approximately thirty million dollars per year with a recent two-year budget set at $61,506,140.

General Conference

The General Conference, presently meeting once every two years, consists of delegates from member states and determines basic UNESCO policy. Although each member may send up to five delegates to the conference, all members possess but one vote. Member states are required by the UNESCO constitution to consult with national UNESCO commissions, when established, and various national educational, scientific, and cultural organizations in the selection of delegates.

Most Conference recommendations require only a simple majority vote, although a two-thirds majority vote is required for: (1) admission of new members, (2) the adoption of an international convention, and (3) the approval of observers from other international organizations and nongovernmental organizations. When the Conference adopts conventions members are required to submit them for possible ratification within one year after the close of the session. Members are also required to have competent authorities consider Conference recommendations. Also, international conferences, relating to UNESCO's field of concern, may be summoned by the Conference.

Members

Membership in UNESCO is open to all United Nations members. Non-United Nations members must gain the recommendation of the Executive Board and approval (two-thirds majority) of the General Conference. Western Germany, Switzerland, South Vietnam, South Korea, and Monaco (as non-UN members) have been admitted under the latter procedure. Entities which are not responsible under international law, such as Mauritius, may be admitted as "associate members," but they are not allowed to vote. UNESCO has 122 full members, including all of the communist states in the United Nations, and three associate members— British Eastern Caribbean Group, Mauritius, and Qatar.

National Commissions

National Commissions are organized groups of persons, normally specialists within the fields of education, science, and culture, formed within member states for the purposes of furthering UNESCO ends by advising delegations to the General Conference and their own governments. They also perform various publication, liaison, and public relations tasks. Although National Commissions are not *required* by the UNESCO constitution, each member state is *requested* to form such commissions and the majority of UNESCO members have done so.

EIGHTEEN-NATION
DISARMAMENT COMMITTEE (ENDC)

The Eighteen-Nation Disarmament Committee was constituted in 1961, after an enlargement of the Ten-Nation Committee on Disarmament, in an effort to bring neutrals and other states into the Committee's work. This Committee has carried the burden of United Nations-related disarmament discussions. There has been a particular emphasis upon ending nuclear tests and preventing the spread of nuclear weapons; although, the hope for some sort of complete disarmament scheme has not been abandoned. Disagreements continue between East and West of the kind which have been present ever since the formation of the Atomic Energy Commission and the Commission on Conventional Armaments. Of particular importance has been the Soviet Union's insistence upon the dismantling of foreign bases in the early steps of disarmament, and the Western emphasis upon an adequate control and verification system, during the phasing out of weapons and forces. Recently there has been considerable interest in the possibility of creating nuclear-free zones, particularly in Latin America and Africa. Although the General Assembly has called for a World Disarmament Conference, Communist China, an important nuclear power, has made it clear that it will not participate in the conference until it is admitted to the United Nations and certain states, i.e., Taiwan, have been expelled.

EXPANDED PROGRAMME OF
TECHNICAL ASSISTANCE

The Expanded Programme of Technical Assistance grew out of an Economic and Social Council request, in February, 1949, that the Secretary-General and heads of the specialized agencies formulate a comprehensive plan to provide technical assistance to underdeveloped areas. Upon the Council's acceptance of the plan, recommendations to establish a program were made to the General Assembly and the Programme became operational, in July, 1950. Prior to this, although the United Nations had engaged in various types of assistance it had been on a very limited scale. The new Programme established a basis for aid in respect to technical assistance, fellowships, training grants, and certain types of material assistance. These activities are qualified, however, by the provisions that a recipient state request aid; decide upon the kind of aid to be given; and cooperate with administering agencies, in respect to such matters as information and publicity. Also, assistance cannot be used to interfere in the internal affairs of recipients.

The Programme has been carried out by a Technical Assistance Board and Technical Assistance Committee.

Various agencies have participated in the program such as UNESCO, Food and Agricultural Organization, International Labor Organization, International Civil Aviation Organization, Inter-Governmental Maritime Consultative Organization, World Health Organization, World Meteorological Organization, International Telecommunications Union, Universal Postal Union, International Atomic Energy Agency, and the Secretariat of the United Nations. Funds are contributed by both United Nations members and other states on a voluntary basis, through pledging conferences, and have been allocated by the General Assembly after recommendations of the Economic and Social Council, Technical Assistance Committee, and Technical Assistance Board. At present, over fifty million dollars are dispensed annually through the program, involving thousands of technical experts, fellowships and grants, and hundreds of programs throughout the world.

In August, 1964, in the interest of coordination, the Economic and Social Council recommended that the Expanded Programme be consolidated with the Special Fund in a new program entitled the United Nations Development Programme (effective January 1, 1966). Although the Expanded Programme and the Fund are to retain their special character as components of UNDP, including separate funds and pledges of monies, they are now coordinated by a thirty-seven nation Governing Council, elected by the Economic and Social Council, and advised by an Inter-Agency Consultative Board (replacing the Technical Assistance Board). The Managing Director of the Special Fund has become the Administrator of the program and the Executive Chairman of the Technical Assistance Board, the Co-Administrator.

Before its merger with the Special Fund, the Expanded Programme had provided technical assistance amounting to over $540,000,000. The 1965–66 program involved over 2,500 projects at a cost of about $98,000,000. (53, 69, 199)

EXPULSION

A state may be expelled from the United Nations by the General Assembly (two-thirds vote) upon the recommendation of the Security Council (veto applies). Presumably, expulsion occurs only when a state "has persistently violated the Principles contained in the present Charter" (Article 6). Oddly enough, the provisions concerning expulsion seem less stringent than those concerning suspension. That is, they seem to allow a greater latitude of application. After expulsion if readmission is sought, presumably, all of the provisions concerning subsequent members apply. Until readmission an expelled member holds the same status as a non-member. That is, certain Charter provisions are still binding upon it. Thus far, no state has been expelled from the United Nations.

FOOD AND
AGRICULTURAL ORGANIZATION (FAO)

The Food and Agricultural Organization came into existence on October 16, 1945, after approval of its constitution by more than twenty states. The constitution was drawn up by an interim commission formed at the United Nations Conference on Food and Agriculture held at Hot Springs, Virginia, in May-June of 1943. FAO became a specialized agency of the United Nations in December, 1946, and reports to the Economic and Social Council. The major purposes of the organization are to foster food and agricultural production, efficiency, consumption, and distribution; further the living conditions of "rural populations"; and contribute, generally, toward expanding the world's economy. In this capacity, FAO collects, analyzes, interprets, and disseminates information and makes recommendations regarding research, education, administration, conservation, processing, marketing, distribution, credit, and commodity arrangements. In addition, it furnishes a wide range of technical assistance including the dispatch of aid missions to assist states in resolving various problems related to the organization's primary functions. FAO has been active in fostering interstate cooperation for the prevention of starvation and has been involved in various projects such as the restoration of land fertility, river basin development, improvement of seeds and fertilizers, and developing preventive measures against numerous diseases connected with agricultural production. Problems connected with forest production and conservation have also been dealt with. The primary organs to accomplish these objectives are the Conference, the Council, and the

Director General (Secretariat). The permanent headquarters are located in Rome with regional offices in the principal geographic subdivisions of the world. FAO publishes numerous materials dealing with projections, trends, and surveys, as well as yearbooks, such as *The Yearbook of Fishery Statistics*.

FAO
Conference

The Conference, which meets in Rome in odd numbered years, is composed of representatives from member states and is the major policy-making body of FAO. It may make recommendations on the numerous matters related to the organization's functions either to individual states, the Council, or to other international organizations. Conventions on FAO matters and amendments to the FAO Constitution must be approved by the Conference prior to submission to member states. The Conference elects the members of the Council, the Director-General, and adopts the FAO budget. Each member state exercises one vote in the Conference.

FAO
Council

The Council consists of thirty-four member states elected by the Conference for two-year terms to act on behalf of the Conference between its sessions. In this capacity, the Council supervises the Secretariat, the regional offices, and the regional and functional bodies. It also makes estimates as to the basic food and agricultural situation and has the right to make recommendations to member states and international agencies in respect to such matters. The Council members always reflect a wide geographic balance.

Director-General and Secretariat

The Director-General, elected by the Conference, operates under the policy guidelines set down by the Conference and the Council and directs the Secretariat, consisting of approximately 3,000 persons. Secretariat members are distributed between the permanent headquarters in Rome and the various regional and sub-regional offices in the world's major, geographic subdivisions. The Secretariat services the other organs of FAO and is involved in numerous technical and assistance functions.

Financing

Once a two-year budget is decided upon by the Conference, member states are assessed according to a scale of contributions based on ability to pay. For example, the United States is responsible for approximately thirty per cent of the budget; while, the United Kingdom has responsibility for ten per cent. The two-year budget for the years 1967–68 amounted to $59,800,000. In addition, FAO spends several millions of dollars as a participant in the United Nations Development Programme.

Members

Membership is open through a simple ratification for those states named in the FAO Constitution, forty-five in all, who served on the Interim Commission producing the constitution. Other states are admitted, upon application, through a two-thirds absolute majority vote of approval by the members of the Conference. The Soviet Union, which served on the Interim Commission, has not chosen to accept membership. Also, certain other communist states, such as Czechoslovakia and Hungary, have withdrawn, although certain non-communist states have also withdrawn, including South Africa which terminated its membership in December of 1964. Presently there are 116 full members and one associate member. The latter, Mauritius, is not viewed as a state and may not vote in the Conference.

National Committees

Many of the members of FAO have formed national committees composed of various officials and representatives of organizations having a bearing on FAO's work. These committees maintain a liaison with the FAO Secretariat and advise their home governments in respect to FAO policies. In addition, they may promote FAO objectives and understanding through publications, meetings, and lectures.

GENERAL ASSEMBLY

The General Assembly is designated as a principal organ by the Charter of the United Nations (Article 7). That is, superficially, it appears to be a co-equal with the other principal organs. In fact, however, it is the central organ of the organization, exceeding all others in importance with, perhaps, the exception of the Security Council in certain matters.

The General Assembly's wide ranging responsibilities are made explicit in Chapter IV of the Charter. The most important provision, Article 10, gives the General Assembly the right to "discuss any questions or any matters within the scope of the present Charter or relating to the powers and functions of any organs provided for in the present Charter, and, except as provided in Article 12, may make recommendations to the Members of the United Nations or to the security Council or to both on any such questions or matters." The General Assembly's right to "recommend," however, stands in contrast to the Security Council's power to "decide" on a number of matters. The qualification referred to in Article 10, regarding the General Assembly's right of recommendation treated in Article 12, concerns a prohibition on the right of the General Assembly to make recommendations in regard to a "dispute or situation unless the Security Council so requests" if the Security Council itself is dealing with the matter. This provision, presumably, makes it impossible for the two organs to work at cross-purposes to one another in respect to disputes or situations. In fact, however, the General Assembly has, at times, taken up and made recommendations on matters which are on the agenda of the Security Council. This behavior has been justified on the grounds that the Assembly is considering a different aspect of the question than the Security Council. In any case, this provision does not prevent the General Assembly from discussing identical questions but merely limits the General Assembly from making recommendations until the Security Council is no longer seized with the matter.

To facilitate the above provisions, the Secretary-General "with the consent of the Security Council, shall notify the General Assembly at each session of any matter relative to the maintenance of international peace and security which are being dealt with by the Security Council and shall similarly notify the General Assembly, or the Members of the United Nations if the General Assembly is not in session, immediately the Security Council ceases to deal with such matters" (Article 12).

Within the above limitations, the right of the General Assembly to make recommendations on collective security matters is clearly affirmed by the second paragraph of Article 11. "The General Assembly may discuss any questions relating to the maintenance of international peace and security brought before it by any Member of the United Nations, or by the Security Council, or by a state which is not a Member . . . [and] . . . may make recommendations with regard to any such question to the state or states concerned or to the Security Council or to both."

In this connection, however, a question sometimes arises as to whether the General Assembly may recommend the use of military force. The last sentence of paragraph 2, Article 11, seems to cause some confusion. It states "any such question on which action is necessary shall be referred to the Security Council by the General Assembly either before or after discussion." If one interprets this to mean military action it appears that the General Assembly is not authorized by the Charter to do more, in respect to the maintenance of peace and security, than recommend measures short of force. This has been the "Eastern" (Communist) interpretation of this provision and has been one basis for the rejection of the Uniting for Peace Resolution.

Another responsibility of the General Assembly is to "consider the general principles of cooperation in the maintenance of peace and security, including the principles governing disarmament and the regulation of armaments, and make recommendations in regard to such principles to the members or to the Security Council or to both" (Article 11, (1)). The General Assembly has exercised this prerogative a number of times, particularly in respect to the problem of disarmament. The most notable case being the General Assembly's acceptance of a version of the Baruch Plan to guide the work of the Atomic Energy Commission.

The General Assembly is also directed to initiate studies, make recommendations, and foster cooperation in respect to international law, human rights, and fundamental freedoms and in the political, economic, social, cultural, educational, and health fields (Article 13). One limitation put on the General Assembly in respect to its studies and recommenda-

44

tions concerning these matters is they must be "without distinctions as to race, sex, language, or religion" (Article 13 (2)).

The General Assembly is also empowered to make recommendations of peaceful settlement in respect to situations detrimental to the "general welfare" and "friendly relations" of states and situations arising from the "violation of the provisions of the present Charter" (Article 14). These provisions, again, seem to imply that the General Assembly should be basically concerned with recommending peaceful adjustments rather than with the employment of force to maintain peace and security.

The pivotal position of the General Assembly is emphasized in Article 15, which requires that the other organs of the United Nations report to it. (The General Assembly, on the other hand, does not report to any other organ.) In the case of the Security Council, the reports must "include an account of the measures that the Security Council has decided upon or taken to maintain international peace and security." One might think that such provisions would open the door to General Assembly scrutiny of Security Council activities. Typically, however, the Security Council's report is accepted without discussion.

The General Assembly's concern with the international trusteeship system (detailed provisions are specified in Chapter XII and XIII) is established in Article 16 and the Assembly must give "approval of the trusteeship agreements for the areas not designated as strategic." (Remaining trust areas, that is, "strategic" ones, are administered by the United States alone and the arrangements are approved by the Security Council.)

Other provisions in Chapter IV treat the budget, voting, sessions, rules of procedure, and the right of the Assembly to create subsidiary organs.

Generally speaking, the General Assembly has vigorously expanded its role and functions over time, almost, at times, to the point of jeopardizing the United Nations, because of the financial obligations incurred. (3, 136, 152, 222)

Additional Items

Additional items are urgent items added to the agenda less than thirty days prior to the regular session or during the session by a simple majority of General Assembly members.

Administrative and Budgetary Committee

The Administrative and Budgetary Committee ("The Fifth") is a main committee of the General Assembly and handles United Nations budgetary questions, including those of the specialized agencies, as well as administrative questions relating to the Secretariat.

Advisory Committee on Administrative and Budgetary Questions

The Advisory Committee on Administrative and Budgetary Questions is a nine member, standing committee of the General Assembly which reviews the Secretary-General's budget estimates and budgetary matters in connection with the specialized agencies and reports to and assists the Administrative and Budgetary Committee. Committee members are appointed for three-year terms by the General Assembly and are selected on a geographic basis and for personal qualifications and experience. At least two committee members must be recognized financial experts and no two members can be nationals of the same state.

Committee on Contributions

The Committee on Contributions is a ten member standing committee of the General Assembly whose function it is to advise the Assembly on the appointment of UN expenses among the members. The scale of assessments formulated by the Committee and accepted by the Assembly is based, basically, on "ability to pay," defined in terms of national income. Once a scale is adopted by the General Assembly it remains effective for a three-year period unless serious factors arise, recognized by the General Assembly, which disturb a state's ability to pay. Members of the Committee on Contributions are appointed by the Assembly, using geographic and merit considerations, for three-year terms with immediate eligibility for reappointment, although no two members can be nationals of the same member state.

Committee on Information from Non-Self-Governing Territories

The Committee on Information from Non-self-Governing Territories was created in 1947 by the Assembly to examine required reports on non-self-governing territories. The Committee was divided equally between states submitting reports and those not submitting reports with the latter elected, for three-year terms, by the Trusteeship Committee (the Fourth) of the Assembly. Procedurally, the reports passed first to the Department of Trusteeship and Non-Self-Governing Territories in the Secretariat, where the information was analyzed, and then to the Committee which, after due consideration, made recommendations to the Assembly concerning the territories, on both procedural and substantive matters, in the economic, social, and educational fields. On

December 16, 1963, the Committee was dissolved by the General Assembly and its functions taken over by the Special Committee.

Credentials Committee

The Credentials Committee is a procedural committee of the General Assembly, consisting of nine members recommended by the President of the General Assembly and appointed by the General Assembly. Procedurally, delegates submit their credentials to the Secretariat which, after an investigation, submits a report to the Credentials Committee which, in turn, reports to the General Assembly. The latter makes a final determination on credential matters. Through this procedure, the GA decides which delegates can legally speak and participate on behalf of their member states in the Assembly.

Economic and Financial Committee

The Economic and Financial Committee ("The Second") is a main committee of the General Assembly and deals with problems and questions implied by its name. This includes concern with the Economic and Social Council and specialized agencies. Its focus upon the broader aspects of world economic developments and standards of living may be contrasted to the more technical work of the Administrative and Budgetary Committee.

Emergency, Special Sessions

Emergency, special sessions are called in the same way as special sessions but are held within twenty-four hours instead of fifteen days of the time of a legitimate request. Unless the General Assembly decides otherwise the item relating to the emergency is immediately taken up in plenary session, without prior reference to the General Committee or a main committee.

General Committee

The General Committee is a procedural committee of the General Assembly consisting of the President, Vice-Presidents, and chairmen of the main committees of the General Assembly. The General Committee is authorized to: (1) review the provisional agenda and make recommendations to the General Assembly, (2) assist the President of the General Assembly in his work, (3) review the progress of the General Assembly, and (4) recommend a closing date for the General Assembly session. Some of these functions have been taken over or are supplemented by informal means (i.e., luncheon meetings).

General Debate

The General Debate occurs at the beginning of each annual session. It consists of a series of speeches, given by delegations wishing to speak, ranging over a wide variety of topics. These speeches tend to stand in contrast to the focus on agenda items in the main committees.

Interim Committee

The Interim Committee, consisting of all member states, was created in November of 1947 by the General Assembly, to meet when the Assembly was not in session.

This innovation, in effect, gave the General Assembly a continuous session existence similar to that of the Security Council. The Interim Committee did make some recommendations and conducted some studies when it was active. One, for example, concerned the use of the veto power in the Security Council. Its real reason for existence was eliminated by the Uniting for Peace Resolution of 1950. It has been adjourned *sine die* since 1955.

Legal Committee

The Legal Committee ("The Sixth") is a main committee of the General Assembly and is concerned with the development of international law and legal questions. The more technical formulations of international law (drafting and codification) are handled by the International Law Commission.

Main Committees

There are seven main committees in the General Assembly of the United Nations. These are: (1) Political and Security Committee; (2) Economic and Financial Committee; (3) Social, Humanitarian, and Cultural Committee; (4) Trusteeship Committee; (5) Administrative and Budgetary Committee; (6) Legal Committee; and (7) Special Political Committee. Each member state is represented on each committee and exercises one vote. A simple majority voting system is used, with one-third of the membership constituting a quorum; although, at least a majority of the members must be present during voting. The main work of the committees is the discussion of agenda items and the preparation of draft resolutions for plenary sessions. Much of the work is facilitated through the use of subcommittees. Each main committee elects its own officers which are the chairman, vice-chairman, and rapporteur. The chairmanship is recognized as a medium and small power (other than the "big five") privilege to offset large power dominance elsewhere in the United Nations. The officer positions are distributed geographically and based on merit.

Plenary Session

Plenary sessions are sessions of the whole which may speak and act officially in the name of the General Assembly. Thus, recommendations and resolutions adopted in plenary sessions have the authority of the General Assembly behind them; while, matters considered and adopted in the main committees and other bodies are work preparatory to consideration in the plenary sessions. In addition, important elections (i.e., those of the non-permanent members of the Security Council and judges of the International Court of Justice) and the General Debate take place in plenary sessions.

Political and Security Committee

The Political and Security Committee ("The First") is a main committee of the General Assembly and handles agenda items such as those relating to peace and security, disarmament, pacific settlement, and the admission, suspension and expulsion of members. It shares its work with the Special Political Committee.

President

The President is the principal, elected officer of the General Assembly. He serves for a session (including special and emergency sessions) and exercises the following functions: (1) opens and closes, through declaration, plenary meetings and (2) directs discussion in plenary meetings with the power to (a) accord the right to speak (always granted), (b) put the question, (c) announce decisions, (d) rule on points of order (may be overruled by the General Assembly), (e) maintain order, (f) propose time and frequency limits on speakers, (g) propose closure on speakers list and debate, (h) propose suspension or adjournment of the meeting, and (i) propose adjournment of debate.

The President is a member of and automatically presides over the General Committee.

In general, the President is an important influence on the course of events in the General Assembly but remains under the authority of the Assembly. If it is necessary for a President to be absent from a meeting he appoints a Vice-President in his place who assumes, as acting President, his powers. If a President resigns or is unable to function a new President is elected. The past President or the chairman of his state's delegation serves at each new session until a successor is elected.

The office of the President is viewed as a "small" power privilege; that is, Presidents are drawn from states other than the "Big Five." (126)

GENERAL ASSEMBLY

Provisional Agenda

The provisional agenda is drawn up by the Secretary-General and distributed to member states sixty days prior to the session. It includes: (1) reports from the Secretary-General and organs of the United Nations, including many of the specialized agencies; (2) items proposed by: member-states (non-member states under certain conditions); principal organs, or the Secretary-General; and (3) budgetary items.

The provisional agenda and supplementary items are scrutinized by the General Committee. The final agenda is determined by a plenary session of the General Assembly.

Regular Sessions

The General Assembly meets every year on the Third Tuesday in September until a closing date set by the Assembly upon the recommendation of the General Committee. Meetings normally take place at the Headquarters in New York, although a majority of members can establish some other meeting place.

Roll Call Vote

A roll call vote is a recorded vote of the General Assembly. Although votes in the General Assembly are normally taken through a show of hands, any state has the right to request a roll call vote. The roll call vote is taken in the English alphabetical order of the names of member states beginning with the member state's name drawn by the President of the Assembly. When a member state is called its representative is required to reply "yes," "no," or "abstension."

Social, Humanitarian and Cultural Committee

The Social, Humanitarian, and Cultural Committee (The "Third") is a main committee of the General Assembly and is concerned with problems and questions implied by its name, particularly in connection with the Economic and Social Council and specialized agencies.

Special Political Committee

The Special Political Committee is a main committee of the General Assembly, sharing the work load of the Political and Security Committee. Because the latter committee was overburdened, an Ad Hoc Political Committee was established to help it during the second session of General Assembly. This committee was re-established on a yearly basis until 1956 when it was made permanent and renamed the Special Political Committee.

Special Session

A special session is a meeting of the Assembly at some-time other than during its regular meeting period. Such sessions may be requested by: (1) a procedural vote of the Security Council, (2) a majority of United Nations members, and (3) a single member of the United Nations if a majority of members concur within thirty days after notification is sent to the Secretary-General. Meetings are to be held within fifteen days of a legitimate request.

Supplementary Items

Member states, principal organs, and the Secretary-General may, at least thirty days prior to the regular session, place agenda items on a "supplementary list," to be considered along with the provisional agenda. The supplementary list must be circulated to members at least twenty days before the session. In the case of special sessions, however, such items may be placed up to four days prior to the session and are circulated as soon as possible.

Trusteeship Committee

The Trusteeship Committee ("The Fourth") is a main committee of the General Assembly and deals with questions and problems connected with the Trusteeship Council as well as non-self-governing territories which are not part of the trusteeship system.

Uniting for Peace Resolution

The Uniting for Peace Resolution was adopted by the General Assembly on November 3, 1950, during the Korean conflict. The United States, France, and the United Kingdom led the drive, in the face of Security Council impotence, to have the General Assembly recommend collective security if the Security Council was unable to do so because of the use of the veto. The resolution was adopted over the objections of the USSR and other Communist states which maintained that the Charter, according to Article 11, paragraph 2, prohibited any organ other than the Security Council from calling for forceful collective security measures. The resolution noted the "failure of the Security Council to discharge its responsibilities on behalf of all of the Member States . . . [and maintained that] . . such failure does not deprive the General Assembly of its rights or relieve it of its responsibilities under the Charter in regard to the maintenance of international peace and security." It then provides that:

> if the Security Council, because of lack of unanimity of the permanent members, fails to exercise its primary responsibility for the maintenance of international peace and security in any case where there appears to be a threat to the peace, breach of the peace, or act of aggression, the General Assembly shall consider the matter immediately with

55

the view to making appropriate recommendations to Members for collective measures, including in the case of a breach of the peace or act of aggression the use of armed force when necessary, to maintain or restore international peace and security. If not in session at the time, the General Assembly may meet in emergency session within twenty-four hours of the request therefor. Such emergency special session shall be called if requested by the Security Council on the vote of any seven members, or by a majority of the Members of the United Nations.

The resolution also established a fourteen-member Peace Observation Commission to "report on the situation in any area where there exists international tension the continuance of which is likely to endanger the maintenance of international peace and security." The Commission can be used by the General Assembly, the Interim Committee, or the Security Council. Each member state was also asked to maintain "national armed forces elements so trained, organized and equipped that they could promptly be made available . . . for service as a United Nations unit or units, upon recommendation by the Security Council or the General Assembly." A fourteen-member Collective Measures Committee was created to "study and make a report to the Security Council and the General Assembly . . . on methods . . . which might be used to maintain and strengthen international peace and security in accordance with the Purposes and Principles of the Charter."

Although the Uniting for Peace Resolution has been employed a number of times in serious international situations since the Korean War—such as during the Suez, Hungarian, and Congo Crises—controversy has continued to surround its use. For example, in the Suez crisis the British and French UN representatives maintained that it was improperly employed because a veto had not actually occurred on the issue at hand before it was invoked. The USSR vigorously opposed its use in both the Hungarian and Congo crises and this opposition, in turn, is related to the USSR's refusal to pay for special financial assessments levied in connection with UN force deployments made during the resolution's use (i.e., Suez and the Congo). In practice, most states have not maintained national military elements for emergency use requested by the resolution and UN forces have been constituted on an *ad hoc* basis in crisis situations (such as the Suez, the Congo, and Cyprus crises).

Vice-Presidents

At the beginning of each regular session the General Assembly elects seventeen Vice-Presidents who have the primary function of serving on the General Committee. The President of the Assembly may ask one of the Vice-Presidents to act in his place if it is necessary for him to be absent. In the interest of geographical balance and other factors, Vice-Presidents are allocated according to the following formula: seven to African and Asian states, one to an Eeastern European state, three to Latin American states, two to Western European and other states, and one to each of the permanent members of the Security Council with the proviso that the election of the President from one of these regions will have the effect of reducing, by one, the number of Vice-Presidencies allocated to it. (Allocation of Vice-President positions to the "big five" stands in contrast to the fact they never obtain chairmanships of Main Committees).

Voting

All questions in the plenary session of the General Assembley are divided into "important" and "other" categories. Article 18 of the Charter specifies important questions as:

recommendations with respect to the maintenance of international peace and security, the election of the non-permament members of the Security Council, the election of the members of the Economic and Social Council, the election of members of the Trusteeship Council . . . the admission of new Members to the United Nations, the suspension of the rights and privileges of membership, the expulsion of Members, questions relating to the operation of the trusteeship system, and budgetary questions.

Questions not listed here automatically fall into the "other" category. However, questions can be moved to the "important" category by a simple majority vote.

"Important" questions are decided by a two-thirds majority and "other" questions by a simple majority. In both cases, ratios are determined by the number of members present and voting. Thus, a large number of abstentions will not prevent a "passing" vote if the proper ratio is met.

A quorum consists of a majority of UN members.

INTER-GOVERNMENTAL MARITIME CONSULTATIVE ORGANIZATION (IMCO)

The convention for IMCO was drafted by the United Nations Maritime Conference sponsored by the United Nations Economic and Social Council, held in February-March, 1948. The convention came into effect in March, 1958 when twenty-one states including the required seven with over one million gross tons of shipping ratified it. IMCO became a specialized agency of the United Nations in January, 1959 following an agreement between the General Assembly and the IMCO Assembly.

The basic purposes of the organization are to promote interstate cooperation on standards of sea safety and technical matters concerning maritime trade and to discourage restrictive and discriminatory trade practices. In this connection, IMCO makes recommendations to states and inter-state agencies; drafts conventions; oversees certain maritime conventions already in effect; sponsors conferences; engages in technical studies, such as those concerning signal codes and tonnage measurements; and disseminates information. The principal organs of IMCO are the Assembly, the Council, the Maritime Safety Committee, and the Secretary-General (Secretariat). The headquarters are located in London.

IMCO
Assembly

The Assembly consists of representatives from all the member states and is the basic policy-making organ of IMCO. Besides establishing the basic work program of the organization, it approves the budget, establishes financial and staff regulations, elects the Council, and approves appointment of the Secretary-General by the Council. The Assembly meets in regular session every two years. On September 14, 1964, the Assembly adopted amendments, subject to ratification, which will increase the Council to eighteen members. Six seats will go to states with the largest interest in shipping services, six seats to states with the largest interest in seaborne trade, and six seats to states with special interests in maritime transport or navigation and whose election will give geographic balance to the Council. Any state which refuses to accept the amendments will lose its membership in IMCO.

IMCO
Council

The Council, consisting of sixteen member states, carries on the work of the organization between sessions of the Assembly and normally meets twice a year. Council members are elected by the Assembly following guidelines to insure that its membership reflects those states with the greatest trade and shipping interests. In effect, these arrangements give permanent seats to states such as the United States, the United Kingdom, and France. Besides supervising the basic work program and the Secretariat, the Council appoints the Secretary-General and drafts recommendations and conventions subject to the approval of the Assembly.

Financing

The IMCO budget, approved by the Assembly, is borne by all members according to a scale of assessments based on the amount of a state's shipping and trade interests. For example, the United States pays the largest proportion, the United Kingdom the second largest proportion, Norway the third largest proportion, and so forth. The 1966–67 budget was set at $1,740,392.

Maritime Safety Committee

The Maritime Safety Committee consists of fourteen member states elected by the Assembly with the specification that at least eight of those elected shall be the largest shipowning nations. The primary function of the Committee is to consider problems of maritime safety problems and make recommendations to the Assembly. The Committee works closely with other international agencies interested in safety, such as the International Telecommunications Union and the International Civil Aviation Organization, and accomplishes much of its work through subcommittees which focus upon certain aspects of maritime safety, such as the carriage of dangerous goods.

Membership

Original United Nations Maritime Conference members and members of the United Nations may become members of IMCO by accepting its convention. Other states may become members by accepting the convention if they receive the approval of two-thirds of the IMCO membership. Western Germany and Switzerland, for example, have been admitted under these procedures. Territories not responsible for their international relations may become "associate members" if the responsible state is already a member. By February, 1967, sixty-four states had become members, including the USSR and the Eastern European communist states with the exception of Hungary and Albania. As in the case of other specialized agencies, the communist states of China, North Vietnam, and North Korea are not members.

Secretary-General (Secretariat)

The Secretary-General, appointed by the Council and approved by the Assembly, supervises the work of a small staff (seventy in 1967) located at the headquarters in London. The primary function of the Secretariat is to perform service, arrangement, and informational functions for the other organs.

INTERNATIONAL
ATOMIC ENERGY AGENCY (IAEA)

The International Atomic Energy Agency came into existence on the 29th of July, 1957, after twenty-six states ratified the statute establishing the organization. This followed an address by President Eisenhower, in 1953, which stressed the need to establish an international agency to further the peaceful uses of atomic energy. The General Assembly unanimously adopted a resolution to establish such an agency in 1954. An international conference—which followed in September, 1956, attended by eighty-one states —unanimously adopted the statute providing for the structure and functions of the organization.

Although related to the United Nations through a special agreement, IAEA is not viewed as a specialized agency. Under the terms of the UN agreement, IAEA reports annually to the General Assembly and the latter may make recommendations in respect to the IAEA regular budget. IAEA has the right, when appropriate, to report to the Economic and Social Council and, if necessary, to the Security Council concerning violations of IAEA regulations relating to the peaceful uses of nuclear material. (Specialized agencies, in contrast, report to and come to an agreement only with the Economic and Social Council.)

The basic purpose of IAEA is to promote the peaceful uses of atomic energy. To further this purpose, IAEA gathers and disseminates technical information, particularly helping less technically advanced nations; facilitates the flow of nuclear materials to those states needing them, by arranging sales and purchases; provides technical assistance with respect to nuclear programs; engages in training and research activity, including the granting of fellowships; organizes and sponsors technical conferences; conducts studies to facilitate the use of nuclear materials; fosters safety standards; and attempts to safeguard against the diversion of nuclear materials to military uses.

In respect to this latter function, the agency has obtained the right of inspection in respect to certain nuclear facilities made available through the Agency. Even in those cases where non-IAEA arranged (bilateral) negotiations have led to the establishment of nuclear facilities, however, the nations involved may request IAEA administration of nuclear safeguards. This is the case, for example, in respect to bilateral facilities agreements between the United States, on the one hand, and Argentina, Austria, China, Greece, Iran, Norway, Philippines, Portugal, Thailand, Indonesia, and South Vietnam on the other. Also, one of the conditions of US nuclear aid to Indonesia (January, 1966), in respect to the Atoms for Peace Program, was to give IAEA inspection rights to insure that the US donated reactor be used only for peaceful, non-military purposes.

There has been considerable pressure to make such practices universal. William G. Foster, in addressing the eighteen-nation United Nations Disarmament Committee in Geneva on January 27, 1966, argued:

> we must continue to secure application of international atomic agency or equivalent international safeguards over peaceful nuclear activities. . . . I urge agreement that all transfers of nuclear materials or equipment for peaceful purposes to countries which do not have nuclear weapons be under IAEA, or equivalent international safeguards.

Also, the Western German government, in March of 1966, transmitted a note to 115 nations calling for, in view of its acceptance of international controls over fissionable materials, similar controls to be exercised by IAEA for all countries outside of the Euratom area.

To facilitate its work, the Agency contacts and works with other agencies dealing in the atomic area—for example, regional ones like Euratom. The Agency is currently responsible for numerous publications including *Nuclear Fission, Atomic Energy Review,* and the IAEA *Bulletin.* The major organs of IAEA are the General Conference, the Board of Governors, and the Director-General. The permanent headquarters are located in Vienna, which is the site of the annual conferences.

Board of Governors

The Board of Governors, consisting of representatives from twenty-five member states, has primary authority and responsibility to carry out the various functions of the organization. The majority of the members of the Board are appointed by a previous Board, according to various criteria. For example, the states most advanced in their atomic technology—the United States, Canada, the United Kingdom, the USSR, and France—are always members of the Board. Certain states which represent the most advanced technology on a regional basis—such as Australia, India, Japan, and Brazil—also, as long as they continue their leadership position, remain members of the Board. Other states are named because they are primary producers of nuclear materials or suppliers of technical assistance. The remaining members of the Board are elected by majority vote by the General Conference with due regard for regional representation. Most decisions of the Board require a simple majority vote, although budgetary matters and appointment of the Director General require a two-thirds majority. The Board meets upon the request of a member state, the Director-General, the General Conference, or on its own initiative. Typically, it meets four times a year at the headquarters in Vienna. In practice, the Board is the central hub of the organization, overshadowing both the Director-General and the General Conference.

Director-General

The Director-General heads the Secretariat of IAEA and operates under the supervision of the Board of Governors. He is appointed for a four-year term by the Board of Governors (two-thirds vote) upon the approval of the

General Conference (majority vote). Members of the Secretariat, numbering approximately 700, are recruited principally for their efficiency and technical competence with due regard for geographic distribution. More than half of the member states have nationals serving on the Secretariat. Under the guidance of the Director-General, the members of the staff are involved in the numerous assistance, information, and research functions of the organization.

Financing

Regular budget expenses recommended by the Board of Governors and approved by the General Conference are borne by the member states, assessed according to ability to pay. In addition, voluntary contributions comprise a general fund used for various operational activities. A recent budget was set at $12,907,000. The organization also receives United Nations monies for its role in the United Nations Development Programme.

General Conference

Each member state of the organization is a member of the General Conference which meets yearly in Vienna. Each member possesses one vote, and a simple majority suffices on all questions except those concerning: the suspension of a member, financial questions, the adoption of amendments, and financial questions, where a two-thirds majority is required. The Conference functions to review the work of the Board of Governors, approve the budget, and approve the reports to the United Nations. The Conference can make recommendations to the Board of Governors and to member states, individually. In practice, the Conference takes the secondary role to the Board of Governors. Special Sessions of the Conference may be convened upon the request of a majority of member states or the Board of Governors.

Members

Any state recommended by the Board of Governors and approved by the General Conference (majority vote) may become a member of the Organization. Members of the United Nations and the specialized agencies were given membership simply by ratification if this occurred within ninety days after approval of the organization's statutes in 1956. Ninety-nine states are members, including the communist members of the United Nations.

INTERNATIONAL BANK FOR RECONSTRUCTION AND DEVELOPMENT (IBRD)

The Articles of Agreement which established the International Bank for Reconstruction and Development were drawn up at the Bretton Woods Conference of July, 1944, and the Bank came into legal existence on December 27, 1945. IBRD became a specialized agency of the United Nations in November, 1947, upon the approval of the General Assembly. The first Bank loan was granted in May, 1947. The Bank had as its original purposes to: aid in economic reconstruction, due to the damaging effects of World War II; further the reconversion of wartime economic facilities to peacetime use; further private enterprise by making loans and guaranteeing loans; and further international trade and productivity. After an initial concentration on European reconstruction, the Bank moved to the broader role of fostering world-wide economic development. In addition to its lending and guaranteeing operations, the Bank supplies advisory service and other forms of technical assistance. For example, the Bank has helped organize survey missions for various countries to facilitate rational long-range development. The Bank may also lend its good offices to help settle disputes over economic matters between member states. The Principal organs of the Bank are the Board of Governors, the Executive Directors, and the President. The headquarters are in Washington, D.C.

IBRD

Board of Governors

The Board of Governors, consisting of one governor appointed by each member state, holds the ultimate power in respect to all phases of the Bank's operations. Governors are appointed for their competence and are frequently former ministers of finance or national bank presidents. The Board meets annually with the Board of Governors of the International Monetary Fund to review operations and establish policy for the Bank. Although most decisions are made by majority vote, voting power is allocated unequally with each Governor receiving 250 votes plus one vote for each share of Bank stock held by his nation state. This enables the developed states, most notably the United States which holds the preponderance of the stock, to dominate the organization.

IBRD

Executive Directors

The Executive Directors consists of eighteen persons, five of whom are appointed by the five largest bankshareholders—that is, the United States, the United Kingdom, France, West Germany, and India—with the remainder elected by the governors of the other member states. The Board of Governors has allocated many of its responsibilities to the Executive Directors who establish operating policy for the Bank. Each elected director commands the votes, as a unit, of the states that have elected him, while appointed directors cast the votes of the appointing state. Such a scheme tends to make the voting power of each director more equal than the voting power of the governors.

Financing

Bank operations are financed, in part, by subscriptions of member states. The Bank's authorized capital, originally $10,000,000,000, was raised to $22,948,300,000 in 1967 and is divided into $100,000 shares, pledged by member states. Two percent of the total pledge is immediately due, either in gold or U.S. dollars. Eighteen percent of the pledge (subscription) may be paid in the member states's own currency and is due upon call. This fraction along with the original two percent comprise the lending fund of the Bank. The remaining portion of the pledge is conditionally due, and may be called, should the Bank need it in order to meet its obligations. Thus far, the Bank has not found it necessary to make a call for this portion of the subscriptions.

In addition to these lending sources, the Bank can and does borrow money and, of course, earns money on its own loans. In fact, the largest fraction of available funds is obtained from various private investors, including life insurance companies and other banks.

A recent administrative two-year budget was set at $34,600,000.

Loans

IBRD loans may be made to governments, political subdivisions of member states, and privately owned economic

68

enterprises within the territory of member states. Loans made to agencies other than a central government, however, must be guaranteed by a central government or a fiscal organ on its behalf.

The Bank is guided in its lending operations by the importance and design of proposed projects, the ability of the borrower to repay, and a condition that the borrower is not able to obtain funds under reasonable conditions from other sources. The terms of the loans depend upon various factors but, particularly, upon the depreciation rate of equipment. Loans up to twenty-five years are frequently made. The interest rate depends, in part, upon the price of money to the Bank itself and, at present, is usually around six percent, one percent of which is a fixed Bank commission.

The Bank has made loans in all geographic areas with the largest fraction going to Asia, the Middle East, and Latin America. In a typical operation, the Bank announced, on January 28, 1966, that it would lend Tunisia fifty-two million dinars to help finance its second Four-Year Plan, the total cost of which was calculated at four hundred, forty-five million dinars.

IBRD

Members

The membership in the Bank is a privilege of any state which has become a member of the International Monetary Fund. States which joined the Fund after December 31, 1945, however, who desire membership in the Bank must be approved by the Board of Governors. Membership may be suspended by the Board of Governors and if not restored within one year the suspended member ceases to be a member of the Bank. The original membership of twenty-eight states has gradually expanded to 109. Yugoslavia is the only member state with a communist government. Cuba withdrew from the organization in November, 1960.

President

The President, elected by the Executive Directors, is the chief executive officer of the Bank and directs its day to day operations. He has the power to appoint and remove the Bank's staff, consisting of over 1,400 persons. The conditions and terms of IBRD loans are recommended by the President to the Executive Directors who must approve them. The President presides over the Executive Directors as chairman and is entitled to vote only in case of tie. The President meets with the Board of Governors but may not vote. All Bank presidents have been US nationals since the Bank's inception.

INTERNATIONAL CIVIL AVIATION ORGANIZATION (ICAO)

The International Civil Aviation Organization came into existence on April 4, 1947, after a sufficient number of ratifications were obtained of the Convention on Civil Aviation (Chicago Convention). The Convention was adopted by the International Civil Aviation Conference of November-December, 1944, attended by fifty-four states. ICAO became a specialized agency of the United Nations in May, 1947, and reports to the Economic and Social Council.

The major purpose of ICAO is to promote international civil aviation, with an emphasis on safety and economy. To accomplish this objective, ICAO: (1) fosters air passage by encouraging state cooperation, planning, and joint support of air facilities, such as weather reporting stations, (2) fosters the preparation of conventions on air traffic matters—such as the Convention on the International Recognition of Rights in Aircraft, adopted by the ICAO Assembly in June, 1948, (3) settles disputes between members in respect to the Chicago Convention, and (4) establishes binding rules and makes recommendations concerning various aspects of air traffic.

The principal organs of ICAO are the Assembly, Council, and Secretary-General. Permanent offices are located in Montreal, Canada, with regional extensions in the world's principal, geographic areas. The organization regularly publishes the ICAO *Bulletin* and *Memorandum on* ICAO as well as a number of technical materials.

ICAO

Assembly

All member states have a right to representation in the Assembly and possess one vote. Most decisions require a simple majority, although an amendment to the Chicago Convention requires a two-thirds majority vote. The Assembly may specify which states' ratifications are necessary before an amendment comes into force and the Assembly possesses the power to deny ICAO membership to a state which refuses to ratify an amendment adopted by the Assembly. Other powers and activities of the Assembly include: (1) election of Council members, (2) determination of the budget, (3) policy recommendations to the Council and member states, and (4) reports to the Economic and Social Council of the United Nations.

ICAO

Council

The Council consists of twenty-seven member states elected for three-year terms by the Assembly with regard to geographic factors and the importance of the role of prospective Council members in respect to air transportation matters. An important function of the Council is the preparation of binding standards, annexed to the Chicago Convention. The Council is assisted in this task by the Air

Navigation Commission, consisting of experts appointed by the Council, whose recommended standards approved by the Council are submitted to member states. Unless a majority of member states reject a standard it automatically becomes part of the Convention and, therefore, is binding on all member states, regardless of their approval. Council recommendations go through the same procedures but are not considered legally binding. Nevertheless, they are considered policy lines that member states are obligated to attempt to conform to. The Council is also empowered to decide disputes between member states over the Convention if negotiations fail and one party brings the dispute to the Council. The Council has the right to call upon member states to deny air space to airlines defying the Convention and can in case of violations deny voting rights to members. In addition, the Council possesses broad investigatory powers.

ICAO
Financing

The regular budget is established by the Assembly. Member states are assessed according to their ability to pay. The United States is responsible for approximately one-third of the regular budget. The approved budget for 1968 was $5,515,000. ICAO also receives United Nations monies because of its participation in the United Nations Development Programme.

ICAO
Members

The Chicago Convention allows World War II allies and neutrals to join the Organization simply by ratification of the Convention. Other states must obtain a four-fifths vote of acceptance by the ICAO Assembly and a majority vote of the General Assembly of the United Nations. One hundred and fifteen states are members, including certain communist states —i.e., Czechoslovakia, Poland, and Yugoslavia.

Secretary-General

The Secretary-General is appointed by the Council, for a five-year term, and supervises, under the direction of the Council, the staff on ICAO, consisting of approximately 500 persons. The Secretariat services the other organs by performing technical, clerical, and informational functions.

INTERNATIONAL DEVELOPMENT ASSOCIATION (IDA)

IDA came into existence on September 24, 1960, as an affiliate of the International Bank for Reconstruction and Development, after a sufficient number of Bank members had accepted its Articles of Agreement. The Association's basic purpose is to promote the economic development of under-developed member states. This is done by a more lenient and flexible financing of projects for underdeveloped states than would be the case if they financed with the International Bank for Reconstruction and Development. Credits may be granted to such states on an interest free, fifty-year repayment plan, in contrast to IBRD's approximately six percent interest rate (including commission) and seven to twenty-five year repayment period. The principal organs of the IDA are the Board of Governors, the Executive-Director, and the President. (267)

Board of Governors

The Board of Governors of IDA is the same, and performs the same functions, as the Board of Governors of

IBRD. When voting on IDA matters the voting power of a governor is basically proportional to his state's subscription to IDA. The US governor, for example, commands approximately thirty percent of all the votes.

Executive Directors

The Executive Directors of IDA are also the Executive Directors of IBRD with similiar functions and voting arrangements.

Financing

IDA's operations are financed primarily through member's subscriptions and certain supplementary contributions made by economically more advanced states. The amount of IDA subscriptions are based upon the amount of subscriptions to IBRD. More advanced states are designated as "Part I" members and pay their subscriptions in a convertible form over a five-year period. Less developed members are designated as "Part II" members and are allowed to pay ninety percent of their subscription in their national currency and the remaining ten percent in convertible currency over a five-year period. Part II members have the right to deny IDA credit grants involving their own currency. By the end of 1965, IDA had granted credits for seventy-nine projects involving over a billion dollars. The only charge on credits thus far has been a service charge of three-quarters of one percent per year, based on outstanding credits. The administrative budget for the 1966–67 fiscal year was $4,466,000.

Members

Membership is open to any state which is a member of the International Bank for Reconstruction and Development.

As of February, 1967, IDA had ninety-six members, only nine short of the full membership of IBRD.

President (Staff)

The President of IDA also serves as the President of IBRD. The various officers and staff below him service IDA in the same way as the Bank.

INTERNATIONAL COURT
OF JUSTICE

Article 7 of the Charter designates the International Court of Justice as one of the "principal organs" of the United Nations while Article 92 defines it as "the principal judicial organ." It operates primarily in the legal sphere. For the most part the court is separated from the mainstream of United Nations politics. Most of the "decisions" of the Court have touched upon matters of minor consequence. Some non-decisional "advisory opinions" have, at times, been directed toward crucial or crisis issues. States may, however, without violating international law, ignore the Court's opinions. Whenever the Court is called upon to render *decisions,* however, states are bound under Article 94 of the Charter to adhere to them and it is possible in cases of non-compliance for the Security Council to recommend or decide upon measures "to give effect to the judgment" (Article 94, **2**). Under present circumstances, states tend to use the Court only when it is convenient for them to do so.

Advisory Opinions

Advisory opinions may be requested by the Security Council and General Assembly, as authorized by the Charter

(Article 96), and by other UN organs and specialized agencies if authorized to do so by the General Assembly. The Court normally honors such requests but has discretion in the matter. Requests, presumably, pertain only to "legal questions." Court procedures during an advisory opinion are similar to those used in judgments. Generally speaking, advisory opinions given by the Court have concerned more important matters than those dealt with in cases leading to judgments.

INTERNATIONAL COURT OF JUSTICE

Advisory Opinion Concerning the International Status of Southwest Africa

In December, 1949, the General Assembly requested an advisory opinion from the Court concerning: the status of Southwest Africa; the obligations of the Union of South Africa in respect to Southwest Africa; the applicability of certain Charter provisions in respect to the Union of South Africa's obligations; and the competence of the Union of South Africa to modify the status of Southwest Africa. This request stemmed from the refusal of the Union of South Africa, which acted as a mandatory under the League in respect to Southwest Africa, to place Southwest Africa under the trusteeship system of the United Nations at the end of World War II. With the founding of the United Nations, all other League mandatories had placed their mandates under the UN trusteeship system making them trust territories. The crucial question in this case concerned whether or not mandate responsibilities continued for the Union of South Africa in spite of the fact that the League and the League machinery concerning mandates had been dissolved. The Court replied, on January 11, 1950, that the Union of South Africa's responsibilities continue under the United Nations, but that UN supervision is limited to the kind of supervision exercised by the League. Further, although the Union of South Africa is not required to place Southwest Africa into the trusteeship system, nevertheless, the Court advised, Southwest Africa's status as a mandate cannot be altered unilaterally by the Union of South Africa.

Advisory Opinion Concerning the Interpretation of Peace Treaties with Bulgaria, Hungary, and Romania

In October, 1949, the General Assembly requested that the Court give an advisory opinion concerning the responsibilities of the signatories of certain peace treaties, concluded in Paris in 1947, and the rights of the Secretary-General of the United Nations in respect to these peace treaties. Under the treaties, Bulgaria, Hungary, and Romania agreed to allow human rights and fundamental freedoms to every person under their jurisdiction. In case of disputes concerning the conduct of the parties arbitral commissions were to be composed. The third member of such commissions were to be appointed by the Secretary-General in case of disagreement between the parties concerning the third member. Although the allied powers claimed that a dispute did exist over the provisions of the treaties, Bulgaria, Hungary, and Romania refused to help constitute any commissions. In view of these events, the General Assembly asked the Court: whether a dispute did in fact exist between the signatories; whether the three states concerned had an obligation to appoint representatives to a commission, and should they fail to do so whether the Secretary-General would have the right to appoint a member; and whether the member appointed by the Secretary-General, in addition to one appointed by the allies, would constitute a competent commission able to make decisions in respect to matters in dispute. The Court advised, on March 30, 1950, that a dispute did exist and signatories were obligated to appoint their respective representatives to a commission. On July 18, 1950, however, the Court advised that the Secretary-General's appointment of a third member was contingent upon the prior appointment of the other commission members. Because the question of the competence of a two-member commission was contingent upon the right of the Secretary-General to appoint one member, the Court did not direct itself to this question.

Advisory Opinion in Respect to Certain Expenses of the United Nations

On December 20, 1961, the General Assembly requested an advisory opinion from the Court concerning the propriety of treating special assessments for peace-keeping operations as expenses of the organization to be "born by the members as apportioned by the General Assembly" (Charter, Article 17, Paragraph 2). This request was precipitated by the failure of several states to pay their special assessments in respect to the peace-keeping operations related to the Suez and Congo crises. The Court advised, on July 20, 1962, that such expenditures properly constituted expenses of the United Nations and, therefore, should be born by the members as apportioned by the General Assembly. The advice, however, had little effect upon the major delinquents— that is, the USSR, France, Belgium, South Africa, Portugal, and several Arab states.

Advisory Opinion in Respect to Reparations Suffered in the Service of the United Nations

In December, 1948, the General Assembly requested an advisory opinion from the Court concerning the right of the United Nations to bring a claim against a government responsible for injury to a United Nations agent to obtain reparations for the United Nations, the agent, or persons related to him. Also, the General Assembly wished to know whether such claims are reconcilable with possible claims possessed by the state of the injured agent. The Court advised, on April 11, 1949, that the United Nations has a right to bring claims on its own behalf for its injured agents and on behalf of persons entitled to compensation due to their relationship with the injured agent. Such claims were not to be viewed as incompatible, in principle, with the claims of the state of the victim and various legal contingencies could be provided for through international agreements. The advisory opinion was precipitated by the assassination of Count Faulk Bernadotte, in Palestine, while serving as a United Nations mediator.

INTERNATIONAL COURT OF JUSTICE

Advisory Opinion in Respect to Reservations to the Genocide Convention

In November, 1950, the General Assembly requested an advisory opinion from the Court concerning the legal consequences of reservations made in adhering to the Genocide Convention. Specifically, the General Assembly wished to know the consequences of possible objections to reservations in respect to the legal obligations between all parties in cases where: states had ratified the Convention; states were signatories but had not ratified the Convention; and states could exercise the right of becoming a signatory but had not done so. These questions were precipitated by the fact that although the Genocide Convention makes no provisions for reservations, nevertheless, a number of states had made reservations in ratifying the convention. The Court ruled, on May 28, 1951, that the legal effect of reservations was not to automatically eliminate a state as a party to the Convention, but, rather, was dependent upon the compatibility of each reservation with the purpose of the Convention. In the case of an objection the state making the objection must judge whether or not the reservations of the reserving state are incompatible with the purposes of the Convention. If it judges that they are from its perspective the reserving state is not a member of the Convention. On the other hand, if the reservations are considered compatible the reserving state may be considered a party to the Convention. In the case of states which are signatories but which have not ratified or which are entitled to sign, but have not signed, such advice becomes applicable only after ratification.

INTERNATIONAL COURT OF JUSTICE

Advisory Opinion in Respect to the Admissibility of Hearings by the Committee on Southwest Africa

In December, 1955, the General Assembly requested an advisory opinion from the Court concerning the compatibility of the practice of allowing the Committee on Southwest Africa the right to grant hearings to petitioners concerning Southwest Africa with the Court's earlier advisory opinion of July, 1950, concerning Southwest Africa. It was the contention of the Union of South Africa that the practice of granting oral hearings exceeded the authority of the General Assembly. The Court ruled, on June 1, 1956, that the General Assembly's practices were consistent with its previous advisory opinion.

INTERNATIONAL COURT OF JUSTICE

Advisory Opinion in Respect to the Competence of the General Assembly Regarding Admission to the United Nations

In November, 1949, the General Assembly requested an advisory opinion from the Court concerning the right of the General Assembly to admit a state on its own into the United Nations in the absence of a recommendation on the part of the Security Council. This request was precipitated by the continuing deadlock and continued use of the veto power in the Security Council in respect to a large number of applicant states. The Court replied, on March 3, 1950, that the Charter requires an affirmative recommendation of the Security Council prior to a decision of the General Assembly to admit a state (Article 4, 2).

INTERNATIONAL COURT OF JUSTICE

Advisory Opinion in Respect to the Conditions of Admission of a State to Membership in the United Nations

In November, 1948, the General Assembly adopted a resolution requesting an advisory opinion concerning the conditions under which a state should be admitted to the United Nations. Specifically, the General Assembly wished to know whether members voting on membership could make their vote contingent upon conditions not specified in the UN Charter and, particularly, a condition that an affirmative vote for one state be linked to affirmative vote for another. This request related to the failure of a number of states to gain admission to the United Nations because members of the Security Council made their votes contingent upon certain conditions of the kind indicated above. The Court replied on May 28, 1948. It maintained that the only proper conditions for admission were those found in the Charter. That is, a state applying for membership should be "peace-loving" and be "able and willing" to carry out Charter obligations (Article 4).

Advisory Opinion in Respect to the Constitution of the Maritime Safety Committee of the Inter-Governmental Maritime Consultative Organization

The Assembly of the Inter-Governmental Maritime Consultative Organization (IMCO) requested an advisory opinion from the Court after a dispute arose in connection with the Assembly's election of the Maritime Safety Committee. According to the constitution of IMCO, eight of the fourteen members of the Maritime Safety Committee should be the largest ship-owning nations. These were designated by the Assembly as France, Federal Republic of Germany, Italy, Japan, Netherlands, Norway, United Kingdom, and the United States. These states were elected to the Maritime Safety Committee by the Assembly. Liberia and Panama, however, have more registered gross tonnage than some of those states designated as the largest ship owning nations. A dispute arose as to whether registration should be the defining criteria of a ship owning nation. That is, it was the contention of Liberia and Panama, in view of their amount of registered tonnage, that they should be included among the eight states elected to the Maritime Safety Committee as largest ship owning nations. Other states maintain that registration was not an adequate criterion, especially because both complaining states allow foreign registration which does not create a genuine connection between them and the ships in question. The Court ruled, on January 8, 1960, that registration was a proper criterion in identifying the largest ship owning nations, and, therefore, the Maritime Safety Committee was improperly constituted in terms of its constitution.

INTERNATIONAL COURT OF JUSTICE

Advisory Opinion in Respect to the Effect of Awards of Compensation Made by the United Nations Administrative Council

During its Eighth Session, the General Assembly requested an advisory opinion from the Court concerning the right of the General Assembly to refuse to give effect to certain decisions of the United Nations Administrative Tribunal. The Tribunal had been created by the Assembly, in 1949, to hear cases relating to the employment of members of the Secretariat. The advisory opinion was precipitated by certain awards made by the Tribunal in connection with members of the Secretariat who had been dismissed by the Secretary-General after their refusal to testify before a US Congressional committee in connection with possible subversive activities. Specifically, the General Assembly wished to know the grounds upon which it could refuse to compensate the individuals concerned in accordance with the Tribunal's decision. The Court ruled, on July 13, 1954, that, as a judicial body, the Tribunal's decisions were final and could not be overruled by the General Assembly.

INTERNATIONAL COURT OF JUSTICE

Advisory Opinion in Respect to the Judgments of the Administrative Tribunal of the International Labor Organization Complaints Made Against UNESCO

In November, 1955, UNESCO challenged certain decisions made by the Administrative Tribunal of the International Labor Organization and requested an advisory opinion from the Court. Arrangements had been made for UNESCO to use the ILO Tribunal in certain cases concerning the employment rights of UNESCO's staff. The request was precipitated by a favorable judgment by the Tribunal for certain UNESCO staff members. Questions were raised, however, as to whether this type of case properly fell under the jurisdiction of the Tribunal. The dispute turned around the right of the Director-General to refuse to renew contracts that had been held on a fixed term basis in light of previously announced administrative procedures. UNESCO was also interested in having an opinion from the Court concerning the propriety of the Director-General's actions, in terms of the good of the service, and the propriety of certain Tribunal announcements. The Court advised, on October 23, 1956, that the Tribunal was within its jurisdiction to hear the cases in question but would not advise on other points in that the statute of the Tribunal, although it allowed the International Court of Justice advisory opinions in cases of a challenge concerning the Tribunal's jurisdiction, did not provide for advisory opinions in respect to the judgments of the Tribunal. The Court advised, however, that because the Tribunal was properly exercising its jurisdiction, its decisions should be considered valid and binding.

INTERNATIONAL COURT OF JUSTICE

Advisory Opinion in Respect to Voting Procedure on Questions Relating to Reports and Petitions Concerning the Territory of Southwest Africa

In November, 1954, the General Assembly requested an advisory opinion from the Court concerning the propriety of voting procedures used in connection with reports and petitions concerning Southwest Africa. The General Assembly had adopted a rule whereby voting on matters concerning Southwest Africa would require a two-thirds majority. It was the contention of the Union of South Africa that the General Assembly's decision concerning voting exceeded its supervisory powers. The Court advised, on June 7, 1955, that the voting rule of the General Assembly was not inconsistent with the guidelines of its previous advisory opinion. To impose a unanimity system upon the General Assembly in respect to such matters would be inconsistent with Charter provisions concerning the Assembly's voting procedures.

Amendments

Amendments to the Statute are made in the same way as amendments to the Charter of the United Nations with the qualification that parties to the Statute who are not members of the United Nations are allowed to participate in the amendment process under rules established by the General Assembly after a recommendation by the Security Council. (Statute, Article 69)

Appeal

Technically, the decisions of the Court are "final and without appeal" (Article 60). However, the Court may "continue" a case upon the request of any party to the case if a dispute arises as to the meaning and scope of a judgment. Also, a state has a right to ask for "revision" if it makes application to the Court within six months of the discovery of a new fact unknown at the time of the case which could have been a decisive factor in the judgment. Such an application cannot be made, however, after ten years of the date of the judgment. The Court, after receiving the application, may open "proceedings for revision" if it agrees that the new fact has the crucial character claimed by the applicant (Article 61, 2).

Aerial Incident of October 7, 1952
(United States claims against USSR)

The United States instituted proceedings before the Court, on June 2, 1955, concerning actions of an aircraft of the USSR against a United States military aircraft off Japan on October 7, 1952. The USSR refused to accept the jurisdiction of the Court and held the United States responsible for the incident. In view of this, the Court ended consideration of the matter in March, 1956.

Aerial Incident of March 10, 1953
(United States claims against
Czechoslovakia)

The United States instituted proceedings before the Court against Czechoslovakia, on March 9, 1955, concerning the behavior of Czechoslovakian aircraft on March 10, 1953, within the US zone of occupation in Germany. Czechoslovakia denied any responsibility and refused to be a party to the case. In view of this, the Court ended consideration of the matter on March 14, 1956.

Aerial Incident of September 4, 1954
(United States claims against the USSR)

The United States instituted proceedings, on August 22, 1958, before the Court against the USSR concerning the behavior of the latter's military aircraft over the Sea of Japan against a military aircraft of the US Navy. The USSR denied responsibility for the incident and refused to give the Court jurisdiction. In view of this, the Court ended its consideration of the case in December, 1958.

Aerial Incident of November 7, 1954
(United States claims against the USSR)

The United States instituted proceedings on July 7, 1959 against the Soviet Union concerning the destruction of a United States military craft over Hokkaido, Japan, in November, 1954. The USSR denied responsibility in the case and refused to view the question open to judicial settlement. In view of these facts, the Court ended its consideration of the case on October 7, 1959.

Aerial Incident of July 27, 1955
(Israel vs. Bulgaria)

Israel instituted proceedings before the Court, in October of 1957, against Bulgaria concerning an aerial incident on July 27, 1955, involving Bulgarian anti-aircraft fire against an Israel airline. Israel claimed that Bulgaria was bound to submit the dispute to the Court's jurisdiction on the grounds that the Bulgarian adherence to the optional clause in 1921 became effective upon Bulgaria's admission to the United Nations in 1955. Bulgaria claimed that she was no longer bound under the provisions of compulsory jurisdiction due to the dissolution of the Permanent Court of International Justice. Although Article 36, 5, of the Statute of the International Court of Justice continues obligations in respect to the optional clause assumed under the old Court, the Court ruled, in May, 1959, that these provisions pertained only to original members, that is, signatories of the Charter, and not to subsequent members. Therefore, the Court was without jurisdiction in this particular case.

Ambatielos Case

On April 9, 1951, Greece instituted proceedings with the Court on behalf of a Greek national, Ambatielos, who claimed damages due to a failure of the United Kingdom to fulfill contractual terms made in 1919 concerning the purchase of steamships. Greece maintained that certain treaties concluded in 1886 and 1926 between Greece and the United Kingdom created an obligation on the part of the United Kingdom to arbitrate the dispute. The United Kingdom maintained that the International Court of Justice possessed no jurisdiction in the case. On July 1, 1952, the Court ruled that it possessed jurisdiction to decide whether the United Kingdom had a duty to arbitrate but lacked jurisdiction to decide upon the merits of the case. The Court ruled, on May 19, 1953, that the treaties in question did obligate the United Kingdom to cooperate with Greece in constituting a Commission of Arbitration.

Anglo-Iranian Oil Company Case

The United Kingdom instituted proceedings before the Court, on May 26, 1951, in connection with the responsibilities of Iran relating to the latter's nationalization, on May 1, 1951, of the Anglo-Iranian Oil Company. The United Kingdom claimed that Iran was obligated to arbitrate the dispute because of an agreement between Iran and the Company in 1933 and because Iran had accepted the optional clause, providing for compulsory jurisdiction, under the Statute of the Permanent Court of International Justice. In view of the fact that Iran was continuing with the nationalization, the United Kingdom requested, in June, that the Court issue provisional measures to preserve the rights of the Company. Such provisional measures were issued by the Court in July and both parties were requested not to take action that would hinder the company or further aggravate the dispute. Iran, however, ignored this order and maintained that the Court did not possess jurisdiction in the case. On July 22, 1952, the Court declared that it was without jurisdiction on the dispute because the Iranian adherence to the optional clause only pertained to *treaties* ratified after her adherence, and that the contract between Iran and the Company did not constitute an international treaty. At the time the judgment was given, the provisional measures of July, 1951, were revoked.

INTERNATIONAL COURT OF JUSTICE—CASES
Antarctica Cases

The United Kingdom initiated proceedings before the Court on May 4, 1955, against Chile and Argentina in respect to certain disputed claims of title in Antarctica. Neither Chile nor Argentina would accept the jurisdiction of the Court and, therefore, the Court ended consideration of the matter.

INTERNATIONAL COURT OF JUSTICE—CASES
The Asylum Case

On January 3, 1949, a Peruvian national, Haya de la Torre, accused by the Peruvian Government of instigating a rebellion, was given asylum by the Colombian Embassy in Lima. The Colombian Government asked the Peruvian Government to give safe conduct to the refugee so that he could leave the country. The dispute over the matter lead to applications to the Court by both parties concerning a number of legal matters. The basic question was whether the behavior of the parties was consistent with treaties between them, in particular, the Pan-American Havana Convention on Asylum, of 1928. The Court ruled in November, 1950, that the Colombian Embassy had improperly granted asylum in terms of the Havana Convention, because of a time difference (too long) between time of the commission of the offense and the time when asylum was sought and, further, that Colombia had no right, in terms of the treaty, to determine unilaterally the nature of an offense for which asylum could be granted. The treaty allowed asylum for political offenses but not for criminal offenses, but such a determination could not be made unilaterally by the state offering asylum. However, in respect to this last point, the Court also pointed out that Peru had not demonstrated that the fugitive properly belonged in the criminal class. Finally, in view of the circumstances and these decisions, Peru was not bound to guarantee safe passage. A request by Colombia on the same day of the judgment as to whether it was bound to surrender Haya de la Torre to Peru was dismissed by the Court on the grounds that new questions were being raised which would require a new case.

INTERNATIONAL COURT OF JUSTICE—CASES

Corfu Channel Case

The Corfu Channel case arose after two British warships struck mines in October, 1946, in the Corfu Channel, which constitutes part of Albanian territorial waters. The United Kingdom presented the case to the Security Council, in January, 1947, after sweeping the Channel of mines in order to acquire evidence. After three months of consideration, the Security Council recommended that the parties refer the dispute to the International Court of Justice. An Albanian objection that the Court did not have jurisdiction was rejected on March 25, 1948. In view of this, the two parties agreed to submit the following questions to the Court: Is Albania responsible under international law for the explosions which occurred on October 22, 1946, in Albanian waters and for the damage and loss of human life? Is there any duty to pay compensation? Has the United Kingdom violated the sovereignty of Albania by reason of the acts of the Royal Navy in Albanian waters on October 22 and on November 12–13, 1946? Is there any duty for the United Kingdom to give satisfaction to Albania?

The Court ruled, on April 9, 1949, that the mines could not have been laid without the knowledge of the Albanian Government and, therefore, Albania was responsible. The Court did not determine, however, whether Albania had laid the mines. Because Albania was ruled responsible, the Court assessed a reparation, on December 15, 1949, of $2,400,000 to be paid by Albania to the United Kingdom.

The Court held that the initial passage on October 22 was an innocent one and, therefore, proper under international law applying to straits. However, the later mine-sweeping activities in November were a violation of Albanian sovereignty. In spite of this, the United Kingdom was not required to give satisfaction to Albania because the Court declaration, itself, constitutes adequate satisfaction.

Albania has refused to pay the assessed reparations.

Case Concerning the Application of the Convention of 1902 Governing the Guardianship of Infants

The Netherlands instituted proceedings before the Court leading to a Court judgment, on November 28, 1958, about the applicability of the Hague Convention of 1902, concerning an infant of Netherlands nationality. It was the claim of the Netherlands that the national law of the infant should be applicable in this case rather than Swedish law, in terms of the requirements of the Convention. The Court ruled against the Netherlands by maintaining that the 1902 Convention did not pertain to the case in question and, thus, Sweden had not committed an international delict.

Case Concerning the Arbitral Award Made by the King of Spain on December 23, 1906

On July 1, 1958, Honduras and Nicaragua, after a prior agreement to do so, submitted an application to the Court concerning a boundary dispute between them. This dispute related to certain boundary decisions by the King of Spain, in 1906, concerning portions of their mutual frontiers. The King's arbitral powers in the case were based upon a convention signed by the two states, in October, 1894, which after drawing boundary lines left disputed points unsettled by other means up to the determination of the Government of Spain. Nicaragua had never been satisfied with the 1906 decisions and the resulting dispute lead to the application before the Court. In November, 1960, the Court ruled that the procedures concerning the award of 1906 were valid and, therefore, the 1906 award was binding upon Nicaragua.

Case Concerning the Barcelona Traction, Light and Power Co., Ltd.

Belgium filed an application before the Court, on September 23, 1958, against Spain concerning some 1948 bankruptcy proceedings in Spain involving the Barcelona Traction, Light, and Power Company, Limited. Because the company in question was owned primarily by Belgium nationals and Belgium considered the Spanish actions to be illegal under international law Belgium asked that the Company's rights be restored and compensation be given. Negotiations between the parties, however, lead the Belgium Government to inform the Court that it was terminating proceedings, and after this was consented to by the Spanish Government the Court ended its consideration of the case in April, 1961.

INTERNATIONAL COURT OF JUSTICE—CASES
(1962 application)

Case Concerning the Barcelona Traction, Light and Power Co., Ltd.

On June 19, 1962, Belgium instituted proceedings before the Court against Spain concerning the Spanish responsibilities regarding the Barcelona Traction, Light, and Power Company, Limited. Previously, Belgium had instituted proceedings in 1958, on the same subject, but had ended proceedings when it appeared that the negotiations would lead to a settlement of the dispute. Under the new application, the Court was asked to determine that Spain had acted illegally under international law and to set the amount of compensation due to Belgium. Consideration in respect to the merits of the case began in July, 1964, after rejection of a certain preliminary objection raised by Spain in respect to jurisdiction.

INTERNATIONAL COURT OF JUSTICE—CASES

Case Concerning the Compagnie du Port, des Quais et des Entrepots de Beyrouth and the Société Radio-Orient

On February 13, 1959, France instituted proceedings before the Court against Lebanon in respect to the compatibility of Lebanese measures against two French companies with the requirements of certain agreements concluded in

1948 between France and Lebanon. The Court ended its consideration of the matter on August 31, 1960, after satisfactory arrangements had been worked out between the parties.

Case Concerning the Northern Cameroons

The Republic of Cameroon instituted proceedings before the Court, on May 30, 1961, against the United Kingdom, concerning the incorporation of Northern Cameroons as a part of Nigeria instead of the Republic of Cameroon. According to the Republic of Cameroon such incorporation was in violation of the Trusteeship Agreement established under the United Nations. In view of the fact that the General Assembly had terminated the Trusteeship agreement and had provided for the incorporation, the Court refused to adjudicate the case on the grounds that any possible Court decision, in terms of the situation, would be without consequence.

Case Concerning the Protection
of French Nationals and Protected Persons in Egypt

A case initiated by France against Egypt concerning the legality of Egyptian measures against the persons and property of French nationals within Egypt was dropped from Court consideration in March, 1950, by agreement of the parties when Egyptian practice was altered to suit France.

Case Concerning Rights of Nationals of the United States in Morocco

On October 28, 1950, France applied to the Court in connection with a dispute with the United States over the rights of American nationals in Morocco relating to treaties between the United States and Morocco dating back to 1836. The issue had been precipitated by a French attempt to apply licensing controls in respect to certain imports, through a decree issued in 1948. Other issues included the extent and application of US consular jurisdiction and a US claim that US consent was necessary before laws and regulations could be applied to US nationals in the French zone of Morocco. Also, the United States claimed immunity for US nationals concerning certain taxes and a system of validation of imports used in connection with customs and assessments. The Court ruled, on August 27, 1952, that: the decree imposing import controls was inconsistent with the treaty responsibilities of Morocco; the United States could properly exercise jurisdiction through the consular courts in respect to civil and criminal cases involving US citizens; the United States could not claim jurisdiction in such cases when the only defendant was a US national or under US protection; and US nationals possess no immunity from taxes unless immunity has been specified in a treaty.

Cases Concerning South West Africa

On November 4, 1960, both Ethiopia and Liberia instituted proceedings before the Court against South Africa concerning the obligation of South Africa in respect to South West Africa. The Court was asked to declare that South West Africa remained a mandate, and that South Africa had violated its obligation as a Mandatory by failing to promote the well-being of the inhabitants in South West Africa because of the practice of *apartheid*. The Court ruled against South Africa's preliminary objections concerning the Court's jurisdiction, on December 21, 1962, and proceeded to consider the merits of the case. In spite of this ruling, however, the Court, on July 19, 1966, dismissed the complaints of Ethiopia and Liberia on the technical grounds that they lacked sufficient legal interest in the case. In its ruling the Court relied upon a "standing" doctrine which requires that states using the Court have a direct, personal interest in the outcome. An unusual feature of the case relates to the fact that the President of the Court used his power to break a tie vote for the first time since before World War II. The fact that this case relates to the emotional topic of *apartheid,* along with the other features indicated above, makes it the most controversial one in the history of the Court.

INTERNATIONAL COURT OF JUSTICE—CASES

Case Concerning Sovereignty Over Certain Frontier Land

Belgium and the Netherlands asked the Court in March, 1957, to settle a dispute between them concerning plots of land on their mutual frontier. Netherlands based its case upon certain agreements made in 1836 and 1841; whereas, Belgium relied primarily upon determinations found in a Boundary Convention of 1843. It was Netherlands' contention that the latter agreement, although giving possession of the plots in question to Belgium, was in error in that, presumably, the determinations made should have been compatible with the earlier agreements. Also, Netherlands maintained that actual sovereignty over the plots in question had been wielded by the Netherlands, rather than Belgium, since the 1843 agreements. The Court ruled, on June 20, 1959, that the 1843 agreement was valid and without error and that the Netherlands claims concerning the exercise of sovereignty were basically unfounded. Therefore, the Court awarded the plots in question to Belgium.

Case Concerning the Temple of Preah Vihear

Cambodia instituted proceedings before the Court on October 6, 1959, concerning Thailand's occupation of the Temple of Preah Vihear, a temple in ruins but of considerable religious significance for Cambodians. Cambodia asked, in its application, for a determination to establish her sovereign rights in respect to the temple area and, also, to have Thailand remove her armed forces from Cambodian soil. After dispensing with Thailand's preliminary objections concerning the Court's jurisdiction, the Court ruled, on June 15, 1962, that Thailand cannot properly occupy the Temple in view of the fact that it is located in Cambodian territory. In addition, the Court ruled that Thailand has an obligation to replace artifacts removed from the Temple during its occupation.

Electricité de Beyrouth Co. Case

On August 11, 1953, France instituted proceedings before the Court against Lebanon concerning the compatibility of Lebanese actions in respect to a French company, the Electricité de Beyrouth Co., located in Lebanon, and Lebanese responsibility in respect to certain agreements between Lebanon and France concluded in 1948. The Court ended consideration of the matter, on July 29, 1954, after the Lebanese Government entered into arrangements with the company that were agreeable to France.

Fisheries Case

In 1935, a Norwegian decree restricted certain fishing grounds off the coast of Norway to Norwegian fishermen and drew the boundaries, for the area concerned, by following lines established in terms of the furthermost headland points on an irregular coast. The United Kingdom applied to the Court, on September 8, 1949, asking it to decide whether the Norwegian procedures utilized were legal and whether damages were due to Britain because of the Norwegian exclusion of British ships from an area which Britain viewed as part of the high seas. The Court upheld the Norwegian position, on December 18, 1951, by deciding that neither Norwegian fishing regulations nor the methods of determining the fishing zones were contrary to international law. In view of these decisions, the United Kingdom has no basis upon which to claim damages.

Haya de la Torre Case

Although technically a separate case, in fact, the Haya de la Torre case grew out of the Colombian Embassy asylum case. When the Court, in the latter case, refused to give an interpretation specifying Colombia's responsibilities in respect to surrendering the refugee, Haya de la Torre, Colombia made a new application to the Court. In view of the Court's previous decision, Peru called upon Colombia to turn over Haya de la Torre and terminate the asylum. Colombia maintained, however, that neither her treaty obligations nor the decision in the Colombian Embassy asylum case dictated this course of action. The Court, basically, upheld the Colombian point of view in rendering its judgment in June, 1951. The Court declared that, although Peru had a legal right to demand termination of asylum because it had been irregularly granted, nevertheless, Colombia was not legally bound to turn Haya de la Torre over to Peru. The Havana Convention, upon which the case partially rested, required the surrender of common criminals but not political offenders. The matter was finally settled through bi-lateral negotiations between Colombia and Peru.

Interhandel Case

On October 1, 1957, Switzerland instituted proceedings before the Court against the United States concerning the US take-over of the shares of the General Aniline and Film Corporation in 1942. The United States justified its behavior on the grounds that although Interhandel, the company owning the shares, was, in actuality, registered in Switzerland, nevertheless, Interhandel, in turn, was controlled and/or owned by I. G. Farbenindustrie which, in 1942, was an "enemy" firm. The Swiss Government, in its application, asked that the Court either rule on the merits of the case or judge that the United States had responsibility in terms of an existing treaty to submit the dispute to conciliation, arbitration, or judicial settlement. The Swiss Government then called for Court provisional measures to prevent the sale of the assets in question. The Court, in October, 1957, denied the need for provisional measures on the grounds that judicial proceedings within the United States would prevent the sale of the assets for a considerable length of time and that the United States had stated that it did not intend to sell the assets in view of the circumstances. On March 21, 1959, the Court ruled against the Swiss application on the grounds that the company in question had failed to exhaust local remedies available to it in the circumstances. Later the Court determined that it lacked jurisdiction, in view of the United

States' terms of acceptance of the optional clause which prevented Court jurisdiction in those cases where the question was one of domestic jurisdiction as determined by the United States.

Minquiers and Ecrehos Case

France and the United Kingdom through a special agreement requested on December 14, 1951, that the Court determine title in respect to the Minquiers and Ecrehos island groups situated in the English Channel. The British and French claims were based on certain medieval treaties and historical facts surrounding the conquest of England by the Duke of Normandy in 1066 and subsequent events. The Court decided, on November 17, 1953, in favor of the United Kingdom, stressing evidences of actual control.

Case of the Monetary Gold Removed from Rome in 1943

Italy instituted proceedings before the Court against France, the United Kingdom, and the United States, on May 19, 1953, concerning gold taken from Germany as the result of World War II. The three states in question had formed a commission to allocate such gold on the basis of a 1946 agreement concerning reparations. The United Kingdom made a claim upon the gold, originally Albanian, to compensate her in regard to a Court judgment in 1946 concerning the Corfu Channel incident. Italy claimed the gold on the grounds that she had suffered damages from an Albanian law nationalizing the Albanian State Bank, which was owned primarily by the Italian state. Albania clalimed the gold on the grounds that it was the property of the Albanian State Bank. The Court ruled, on June 15, 1954, that it lacked jurisdiction in the matter because to decide such a case required consent which had not been given. For this reason, the Court could not decide between the claims of Italy and Albania on the one hand or Italy and the United Kingdom on the other.

Case of Certain Norwegian Loans

France instituted proceedings in 1957 against Norway concerning her obligations in respect to loans floated by Norway in France between the years 1885 and 1909. France maintained that the terms of the loans required payment in gold or certain other gold convertible currencies, rather than Norwegian kröner, because kröner was no longer convertible to gold. The Court ruled on July 6, 1957, that it lacked jurisdiction in the case because of the Norwegian right to invoke, by reason of reciprocity, certain French reservations in respect to its acceptance of the Court's jurisdiction under the optional clause.

Nottebohm Case

Liechtenstein, on December 17, 1951, instituted proceedings before the Court against Guatemala on behalf of Frederick Nottebohm who had been naturalized by Liechtenstein in October, 1939. Originally Mr. Nottebohm had been a German national but had been living, for the most part, in Guatemala since 1905. Nottebohm's claims concerned the application of war measures against Nottebohm's person and property by Guatemala in 1943. Guatemala contested Liechtenstein's suit, however, on the grounds that the 1939 naturalization process had not conferred the status of a "neutral person" on Nottebohm, because of the tenuous length between Nottebohm and Liechtenstein. Also, Guatemala denied that the Court currently had jurisdiction because Guatemala's original acceptance of the optional clause expired in January, 1952, before the Court could give a judgment in the case. The Court ruled, in November, 1953, that it had jurisdiction because the Court had been seized with the matter prior to the expiration date of the optional clause. In April, 1955, it ruled against Liechtenstein, maintaining that the circumstances under which nationality had been granted were insufficient to enable Liechtenstein to present a claim on behalf of Nottebohm.

Right of Passage over Indian Territory Case

Portugal instituted proceedings before the Court on the grounds that in July, 1954, the Indian Government prevented Portugal's lawful right of passage to and between the Portuguese enclaves of Dadra and Nagar-Aveli located in Indian territory. The Portuguese claim was based upon: certain agreements concluded in the eighteenth century; actual practice over time in respect to the enclaves; and international custom in respect to such situations. A claim by India that the Court did not possess jurisdiction was rejected by the Court, in November, 1957. In April, 1960, the Court decided that Portugal had the right of legal passage to and between the enclaves but that this right was circumscribed and did not include the right of passage in respect to arms, ammunition, armed police, and armed forces. The Indian behavior in terms of these limitations was found to be legal.

Treatment in Hungary of Aircraft and Crew of United States of America

The United States instituted proceedings before the Court, on March 3, 1954, against Hungary and the USSR concerning the treatment of a US aircraft and its crew forced to land in Hungary. Both the USSR and Hungary refused to give the Court jurisdiction in the matter and blamed the United States for the incident. The Court ruled, in July, 1954, that it lacked jurisdiction, in view of the attitudes of Hungary and the USSR.

INTERNATIONAL COURT OF JUSTICE

Composition

Fifteen judges are elected to the Court for nine-year terms (staggered, five judges every three years) by absolute majorities in the Security Council and General Assembly, voting independently of one another. However, elections are subject to the proviso that no two elected judges be of the same nationality and the Court, as a whole, represent "the main forms of civilization and of the principal legal systems of the world" (Statute, Article, 9). If the voting process gives concurrent absolute majorities to more than one national of a single state only the oldest judge is considered elected. Judges are nominated by national groups used in connection with the Permanent Court of Arbitration. If, however, a state is party to the Statute of the Court but not a member of the Permanent Court judges are nominated by specially appointed persons in the states concerned. All nominations are to be made from persons "of high moral character, who possess the qualifications required in their respective countries for appointment to the highest judicial office, or are jurisconsults of recognized competence in international law" (Statute, Article 2). National, nominating groups are limited to naming four persons, no more than two of whom can be of the nominating group's own nationality.

Should the election process fail to fill all the seats the elected members of the Court are empowered to do so, within a period fixed by the Security Council, from those candidates which have already received votes in either the General Assembly or the Security Council, with the proviso that a joint conference of representatives of the Security Council and General Assembly (three members from each) should first have attempted to get acceptance by the two organs of candidates selected by the conference.

All permanent members of the Security Council have been represented by election on the Court since its existence, but "big five" judges possess no special privileges. If a party to a dispute does not have a judge of its own nationality on the Court, it may choose one for the case even though, presumably, judges are "elected regardless of their nationality." (Compare: Statute Articles 2 and 3). While persons are serving as judges they are forbidden from holding any other political, administrative, or professional position.

INTERNATIONAL COURT OF JUSTICE

Enforcement

As is universally the case with courts, the International Court of Justice has no means of its own to enforce its own judgments. However, "if any party to a case fails to perform the obligations incumbent upon it under a judgment rendered by the Court, the other party may have recourse to the Security Council, which may, if it deems necessary, make recommendations or decide upon measures to be taken to give effect to the judgment" (Charter, Article 94 (2)). The permanent members of the Security Council, however, stand in a different, legal position than other members of the international community on the matter of the enforcement of Court judgments in that they possess the veto power in the application of Article 94, even in their own case. In one case of a clear violation of a Court judgment since World War II, where Albania refused to pay damages in the Corfu Channel case, the injured party, Great Britain, did not appeal to the Security Council. States, individually, of course, may still apply sanctions in such cases of failure to adhere to Court judgments if such action is not prohibited by the United Nations Charter.

Judicial Decisions and Teachings of Publicists

Judicial decisions and teachings of highly qualified publicists are designated by the Statute of the International Court of Justice as "subsidiary means for the determination of the rules of law." Many authors have noted the impact of publicists upon the rules of international custom, related to the fact that judges tend to rely upon the writings of publicists in ascertaining the content of customary law. Basically, then, this Statute provision reaffirms this practice by judges.

The use of judicial decisions to clarify rules, on the other hand, is somwhat obscured by other provisions in the Statute. Article 59 forbids, in effect, the use of the rule *stare decisis* (considering the decisions of previous cases binding in respect to present cases). However, to the extent that the judges do look to previous cases to clarify rules, it would seem that this activity should shape their decisions in the particular case under consideration.

INTERNATIONAL COURT OF JUSTICE

Jurisdiction

The Court has jurisdiction when disputes are referred to it by states (consent of all parties); treaties confer jurisdiction; and parties to a dispute have previously declared themselves bound by the "optional clause" concerning certain categories of cases. Thus, *consent* is assumed in all cases prior to the actual exercise of jurisdiction by the Court. However, "in the event of a dispute as to whether the Court has jurisdiction, the matter shall be settled by the decision of the Court" (Article 36-6). In practice, this right of the Court appears to be partially undercut by the character of reservations adopted by states in accepting the "optional clause." If the Court does decide it has jurisdiction failure to appear by one of the parties cannot prevent an unfavorable judgment. That is, "whenever one of the parties does not appear before the Court, or fails to defend its case, the other party may call upon the Court to decide in favor of its claims" (Statute, Article 53-1). However, the claim itself, in such a case, must be "well founded in fact and law" (Article 53-2).

INTERNATIONAL COURT OF JUSTICE
Law Applied

When deciding disputes the Court, by provision of Article 38, is allowed to apply: (1) "international conventions, whether general or particular, establishing rules expressly recognized by the contesting states," (2) "international custom, as evidence of a general practice accepted as law," (3) "general principles of law recognized by civilized nations," and as "subsidiary means" for the determination of the rules of law, (4) "judicial decisions and the teachings of the most highly qualified publicists" with the proviso that decisions have "no binding force except between the parties and in respect . . . [to a] . . . particular case" (Article 59). The Court can, however, decide a case *ex aequo et bono* if the parties to the case so agree.

INTERNATIONAL COURT OF JUSTICE
Members of

All members of the United Nations are automatically parties to the Statute of the International Court of Justice and therefore members of the Court (Charter, Article 92). A state not a member of the United Nations that wishes to become a member of the Court may do so upon the recommendation of the Security Council upon conditions established by the General Assembly. For example, Switzerland, San Marino, and Liechtenstein have become members of the Court on the conditions that they accept the provisions of the Statute of the Court and Article 94 of the Charter, requiring compliance with Court decisions, and contribute to the expense of the Court.

"Optional Clause"

The "optional clause" refers to Article 36, **2,** of the Statute of the Court. It provides that the Court will have jurisdiction in respect to: interpretations of treaties; questions of international law; the existence of facts relating to breaches of international obligations; and the nature and extent of reparations for breaches of international obligations. Jurisdiction is qualified, however, by the stipulation that it applies in cases where the disputing parties indicate, through prior declaration, that they wish the Court to have jurisdiction in such matters, "in relation to any other State accepting the same obligation." Thus, each state is obligated through its declaration to recognize the Court's jurisdiction in such matters in respect to every other state accepting the same obligations. States, however, may attack "reservations" to their optional clause declarations. Reservations have been varied and numerous. The United States, for example, exempts from Court jurisdiction: (1) disputes entrusted to other tribunals by prior or future agreement, (2) disputes within the "domestic jurisdiction" of the United States as determined by the United States, and (3) disputes involving multilateral treaties unless all signatories are parties to the case or the United States agrees to confer jurisdiction. Similar declarations by other states have greatly reduced the significance of Article 36, **2,** and **6,** which provide that "in the event of a dispute as to whether the Court has jurisdiction, the matter shall be settled by the decision of the Court." The fact that states may make dissimilar declarations and require reciprocity provides a basis for the Court excluding the application of the "optional clause" in certain cases on the grounds that both parties have not accepted "the same obligation." Thus, a state, in attempting to press a claim based on the optional clause, may find that its own reservations provide a basis for a counter-claim, which may be accepted by the Court, that the optional clause cannot be applied. Finally, some states have reservations providing for immediate termination of the optional clause obligations or immediate extensions of reservations which, for practical purposes, may allow them to escape an obligation for legal settlement in *any* dispute. As of June 30, 1966, forty-two states were "bound" by "optional clause" declarations. (Since August 14, 1951, the US declaration may be terminated upon six months ratification.)

INTERNATIONAL COURT OF JUSTICE
Provisional Measures

The Court has the right to call for provisional measures in a case if such measures are necessary to protect the rights of either party. For example, the Court issued such measures in the *Anglo-Iranian Oil Company Case* (1951), involving the Iranian nationalization of a British oil company, when it called upon the parties to restrain themselves from action that would aggravate the dispute or be harmful to the company (i.e., the pre-nationalization management was to continue). Such Court measures are binding upon states and, therefore, have the same status as decisions, in contrast to recommendations. In the above case, however, Iran ignored the provisional measures.

INTERNATIONAL COURT OF JUSTICE
Quorum

When the full Court sits nine judges constitute a quorum. However, the Court may divide into chambers of three or more judges to deal with certain categories of cases (i.e., labor cases) or form a special chamber for a certain case if the parties to the case agree. Also, the Court forms annually a chamber of five judges, which if the parties to a case so desire hears cases with simplified procedures. Whenever a decision is reached with any of the above arrangement it has the full authority of the Court.

Statute

The Statute of the Court, after being drafted by the United Nations Committee of Jurists, was accepted at the San Francisco Conference as an integral part of the Charter of the United Nations. There is no way, therefore, for a state to be a member of the United Nations and not be a member of the Court; although, the Statute may be adhered to by states that are not members of the United Nations. The Statute has the same status as any treaty and, therefore, is considered binding. Its seventy Articles provide for the Court's organization, competence, procedures, and the amendment procedures to be employed in changing the Statute. Basically, the provisions are similar or the same as those which created the Permanent Court of International Justice.

Use

The Court may be used by all members of the United Nations and non-members under conditions laid down by the Security Council. The Security Council is forbidden, however, from establishing conditions for non-members that would place such states "in a position of inequality before the Court" (Statute Article 35, 2). The Security Council has required non-members that wish to use the Court to indicate through a declaration to the Registrar of the Court that they will comply with the Statute and rules of the Court in accepting the Courts jurisdiction and be bound by the decisions of the Court. The contribution for Court expenses when non-members use the Court is determined by the Court (Article 35, **3**).

INTERNATIONAL COURT OF JUSTICE

Voting

Decisions of the Court, when legally constituted, are made by a majority of the judges *present,* with the President or the judge acting for the President casting the deciding vote in case of a tie. It should be noted that this system differs from a simple majority system based upon those *present and voting,* as used by the General Assembly. Each judge has the right to present a separate opinion concerning a decision of the Court.

INTERNATIONAL FINANCE CORPORATION (IFC)

The International Finance Corporation, founded on July 20, 1956, is affiliated with but is legally separate from the International Bank for Reconstruction and Development. The primary function of the Corporation is to further private enterprise in underdeveloped nations. This is accomplished by IFC investment in cooperation with private capital in various projects, such as mining and manufacturing, where private capital is insufficient. Private investment is also facilitated through research and information dissemination concerning possible economic opportunities and the soundness of projects. Investments are limited to private enterprises located within member states. Member governments need not guarantee, in projects concerning their nationals, repayment of investments to the Corporation, should a project fail. A member government may prevent, however, investments in its jurisdiction by IFC. As a specialized agency of the United Nations, the Corporation reports to the Economic and Social Council. Its principal organs are the Board of Governors, the Board of Directors, and the President. The headquarters are located in Washington, D.C.

IFC
Board of Directors

The Board of Directors of IFC consists of those directors of the International Bank for Reconstruction and Development representing countries that belong to IFC. The Board plays the same role as it does in the case of IBRD and elects the President of IFC.

IFC
Board of Governors

The Board of Governors is composed of the governors of the International Bank for Reconstruction and Development whose countries hold membership in IFC. The functions of the Board are similar to those of IBRD and meetings are held simultaneously with board meetings of the Bank and the International Development Association.

IFC
Financing

The operations of IFC are financed through subscriptions made by member states, earnings from investments, and borrowed funds. Capital is authorized at $100,090,000. As in the case of the International Bank for Reconstruction and Development, the size of the country's subscription determines its voting power. Thus, the United States, with the largest subscription, commands approximately thirty percent of the total vote. By the end of the fiscal year 1966, IFC's activities embraced gross commitments of over $204,000,000. A recent two-year administrative budget was set at $3,053,245.

IFC

Members

Membership in IFC is an optional privilege of the members of the International Bank for Reconstruction and Development. Eighty-seven of the Bank members have become members of the Corporation.

IFC

President

The President of IFC, elected by the Board of Directors, plays the same role as the President of the International Bank for Reconstruction and Development. In fact, the same person has served both positions. In contrast to the International Development Association, however, IFC has a small but separate staff from that of IBRD.

INTERNATIONAL
LABOR ORGANIZATION (ILO)

ILO was created in 1919 by the Treaty of Versailles as an autonomous organization associated with the League of Nations. In 1946, after constitutional amendments, it became the first specialized agency of the United Nations reporting to the Economic and Social Council. ILO's basic purpose is to further "social justice" as a contribution to international peace. ILO's constitution specifies concern with numerous matters including hours of work, unemployment, workers' health, child labor, old-age security, freedom of association, and educational matters. The aims of the organization were further specified in the Declaration of Philadelphia, adopted at an ILO conference in 1944. This declaration includes concern with standards of living, fitting persons to occupations, labor mobility, policy development in respect to hours and wages, extending the right of collective bargaining, equality of opportunity, and problems connected with nutrition, housing, recreation, and child welfare. A primary concern of ILO is to establish an International Labor Code. In addition, ILO renders various types of services and technical assistance.

The principal organs are the International Labor Conference, the Governing Body, and the Director-General (International Labor Office). The central headquarters are in Geneva, Switzerland, with branch offices in cities such as London, Rio de Janeiro, Rome, and Washington. ILO is responsible for numerous publications, many of a technical nature concerning such matters as unemployment, wages, prices, etc. It also publishes a monthly *International Labor Review,* a quarterly magazine entitled *I. L. O. News,* and a yearly summary of statistics entitled *Yearbook of Labor Statistics.*

ILO

Director-General

The Director-General appointed by the Governing Body is the chief executive officer of ILO, playing a role similar to the Secretary-General of the United Nations, with responsibility for the International Labor Office and its Secretariat, located in Geneva. The Director-General is responsible for the recruitment and appointment of his staff, who service the various organs of ILO in a secretarial and technical fashion and carry out programs determined by the International Labor Conference and the Governing Body. There are approximately 2,000 staff members including 650 technical experts in the field. The Director-General is also responsible for the Annual Report which provides a discussion focal point for the yearly International Labor Conference.

Financing

The principal source of revenue for the Organization is from member states who are assessed using a scale of contributions applied to a yearly budget ($25,634,000 was recently approved) by the International Labor Conference. The United States is the largest contributor, having responsibility for twenty-five percent of the budget. ILO also receives funds by participating in the United Nations Development Programme.

Governing Body

The Governing Body is the principal executive organ of ILO consisting of forty-eight members—twenty-four of which represent governments, twelve of which represent employers, and twelve of which represent workers. Ten governments of "primary" industrial importance are permanently represented. These are: Canada, China, France, Western Germany, India, Italy, Japan, USSR, United Kingdom, and the United States. Non-permanent governmental members are elected by permanent governmental representatives. The employer and worker members are elected by their respective groups in the International Labor Conference, excepting those representatives whose governments have permanent seats. The Governing Body normally meets three times a year and appoints the Director-General; makes preparations for the Labor Conference, including agenda composition; and reviews the budget prior to its submission to the Conference. (The budget is initially drawn up by the

Director-General.) The Governing Body is also concerned with policy directives to the International Labor Office.

International Labor Code

The International Labor Code consists of over 200 conventions and recommendations which have been adopted by the International Labor Conference. Conventions are binding upon states that have accepted them. Should a worker or employer organization feel that a particular convention is not being applied it may file a complaint with the International Labor Office. The Governing Body may then decide to publish the facts of the case for the scrutiny of other members. Should a member state feel that another member state has violated a convention a Commission of Inquiry may examine the matter and make recommendations. Although states are not bound by recommendations and unratified conventions, nevertheless, states are bound to give information to the Governing Body concerning the reasons why ratification of a Conference adopted convention has not been completed and, also, in cases where there has been a failure to implement Conference recommendations. The Code covers a wide variety of matters including treatment of migrants, maximum hours of work, holidays, old-age insurance, contract clauses, rights of association, and minimum wages.

International Labor Conference

The International Labor Conference, which meets yearly at Geneva, is the basic policy making organ of ILO consisting of four voting delegates from each member state. The delegates are appointed so that two of them represent the member government, one represents the employers, and one

115

represents the workers of a member state. The selection of employers' and workers' representatives are made by member governments in consultation with representative organizations of workers and employers. For example, in the case of the United States, the US Chamber of Commerce submits employers nominations considered by the government. During the Conference delegates divide along governmental, employer, and worker lines for organizational and certain elective purposes.

The primary work of the Conference is to establish an International Labor Code which consists of both conventions and recommendations adopted by a two-thirds vote of the Conference. Conventions adopted by the Conference become effective after state ratification and member governments are "obligated" to submit each convention to the ratification process, even though it may not be successfully ratified. Recommendations that have legislative implications must be submitted by member governments to appropriate organs for possible action. Member governments are also obligated to report to ILO on the implementation of the conventions and recommendations. A Commission of Inquiry may hear complaints concerning failure of a state to live up to a convention that it has ratified.

One of the primary problems of the Conference has been to adjust its requirement that employers be represented to the fact that a number of member states no longer have private employers, due to extensive nationalization (i.e., communist states).

ILO

Members

Membership in ILO is not automatic but rather "optional." This option may be exercised by UN members by notification of the Director-General of ILO. The bulk of the United Nations members, including Communist states, are presently members of ILO. Albania, however, on August 5, 1965, notified ILO of its decision to withdraw. There are presently 118 members.

INTERNATIONAL LAW COMMISSION

The International Law Commission was created by the General Assembly in November, 1947. It originally consisted of fifteen legal experts, elected for five-year terms. Since that time, the Commission has been expanded to twenty-five members. Commission members are nominated by United Nations members and elected by the General Assembly with the stipulation that no two members be of the same nationality and that they represent the main forms of civilization and the major legal systems of the world. Because the Commission members function as experts they may not receive instructions from states concerning their work. Their primary task is to develop and codify international law. This does not mean that the Commission can "create" international law, however, rather, the Commission attempts to draft what it considers to be the essence of international practice. A typical codification "cycle" is for draft codes to go from the Commission to the General Assembly for approval; to states, for commentary; back to the Commission; to the General Assembly; and, finally, to an international conference for adoption. For example, this was the basic cycle in regard to the United Nations Conference on Diplomatic Intercourse and Immunities held in Vienna in March–April, 1961, leading to the adoption of the Vienna Convention on Diplomatic Relations.

The basic direction of the Commission's work was established by its first session, in 1949, when it listed various areas subject to codification—including the law of treaties, arbitral procedures, counselor intercourse and immunities, succession of states and governments, jurisdiction in respect to the high seas and territorial waters, the treatment of aliens, diplomatic intercourse and immunities, recognition of states and governments, statelessness, and state responsibilities. Considerable progress has been made in these areas and others, in the sense that the Commission has produced a number of draft codes and made numerous recommendations to the General Assembly.

In addition to this work, the Commission may produce draft "declarations" which have a bearing upon international law but which do not constitute international law. In this category is the Commission's Draft Declaration on Rights and Duties of States, prepared in 1949. The Declaration includes such state rights as "independence" and "equality." The General Assembly has brought this Declaration to the attention of member states and jurists.

The Commission has also enunciated "principles" in connection with the Nuremberg Judgments (by asserting that persons may be responsible for illegal acts under international law that are not illegal under national law) and by defining as punishable under international law crimes against the peace, war crimes, and crimes against humanity.

However, until such "declarations" and enunciations of "principles" are accepted in international conventions their moral character is more evident than their legal character.

The Commission's work is summarized in the *Yearbook of International Law Commission*. Other information, of a documentary character, can be found in the *Official Records* of particular sessions. The Commission normally meets in Geneva for three to four month, annual sessions. (147)

INTERNATIONAL
MONETARY FUND (IMF)

The International Monetary Fund came into existence on December 27, 1945, when a sufficient number of states had ratified its Articles of Agreement. The Articles were drawn up by the United Nations Monetary and Financial Conference (Bretton Woods Conference) of July, 1944. IMF became a specialized agency of the United Nations in November, 1947, and reports to the Economic and Social Council.

IMF'S primary purposes are to foster international monetary cooperation, international trade, and exchange stability. It does this by establishing a multi-lateral system of payments to assist in the elimination of foreign exchange restrictions and by attempting to promote currency stability by making Fund resources available to members under suitable safeguards. In addition, the organization provides technical advice and assistance to members in respect to monetary matters.

Recently, considerable progress in the establishment of a multilateral system of payments has been made because a number of members have accepted obligations under "Article VIII", which limits restrictive innovations in respect to exchange rates and currency practices upon consent of the IMF.

One of the most important services of the Fund is to allow members to charge purchases of one another's currency. This promotes currency stability and helps adjust for temporary imbalances in the payments situation.

The principal organs of the Fund are the Board of Governors, the Executive Directors, and the Managing Director. The headquarters are located in Washington, D.C. IMF publications include *International Financial Statistics, Balance of Payments Yearbook, International Financial News Survey,* and an *Annual Report.*

IMF

Board of Governors

Each member state is entitled to one governor and one alternate governor on the Board of Governors. The function of the alternate governor is to act for the governor in his absence. Each governor wields two hundred and fifty votes plus additional votes, depending upon the size of his country's contributions to IMF resources. This system gives the developed states a dominant voice in the organization. For example, the US governor commands something over twenty percent of the vote, the United Kingdom's governor around twelve percent, Western Germany's governor four percent, and so forth. The Board normally meets once a year and decides most questions by a simple majority vote. Although the Articles of Agreement place all power over IMF affairs in the hands of the Board, in practice, the Executive Directors make most of the important decisions.

IMF

Executive Directors

The Executive Directors decide upon policy in respect to the operations of the Fund. The United States, the United Kingdom, France, Western Germany, and India, by virtue of the size of their quota to IMF, are each allowed to appoint one director. The remaining directors are elected by the Board of Governors. Each elected director casts the votes of those states which elected him. The Directors meet as the occasion requires and are considered as being in "continuous session." Numerous technical decisions, such as those concerning convertibility, constitute a large fraction of the Executive Directors' work load.

IMF

Financing

Administrative costs, $22,100,000 are met by a budget approved by the Board of Governors. Income from charges and returns from investments normally exceed these costs.

Fund operations, on the other hand, utilize Fund resources derived from subscriptions from member states, based upon quotas. Quotas for original members were initially set in the Articles of Agreement at the Bretton Woods Conference. The Board of Governors establishes quotas for other states as they come in to IMF. Quotas may be revised by a four-fifths vote of the Board of Governors and become effective upon the consent of those members who together subscribe two-thirds of the total quota amount. A recent proposed revision will bring Fund resources to twenty-one billion dollars. Members are required to pay twenty-five percent of their quota in gold and the remaining seventy-five percent in their national currency. This is the case unless this requirement forces a state to divest itself of more than ten percent of its net dollar-gold holdings. In such a case, the state concerned pays up to the ten percent "limit" and then meets the remainder of its quota with its own national currency. The effect of this rule is to allow poorer states to pay a greater proportion of their quota in their own currency. In addition to these resources, the Fund has negotiated agreements with ten of its most advanced industrial members to lend up to six billion dollars to correct or prevent serious disruptions of the international monetary system.

IMF

Managing Director

The Managing Director is the principal executive officer of the Fund. He executes the policy of the Executive Directors and the Board of Governors. The Director is elected for a five-year term by the Executive Directors and is in charge of a staff of over 800 persons drawn from member states on the basis of merit and wide geographic distribution. The staff is responsible for handling the business of the Fund which includes research, consultation, and publication activities.

Members

The states that were present at the Bretton Woods Conference of 1944 possessed the right of membership if they ratified the Articles of Agreement prior to December 31, 1945. Membership since then has been open to any state which, after application, can secure a simple majority of the total votes cast by the Board of Governors. The present membership (105) includes the bulk of United Nations members and certain non-UN members states, such as Western Germany and South Vietnam, but does not include the USSR, Communist China, or the communist states of Eastern Europe with the exception of Yugoslavia.

Par Value

The par value of a currency is its value expressed as a ratio with another currency or with gold. All Fund member currencies are expressed in terms of US dollars and/or gold. Once a par value has been agreed upon between a member state and the Fund significant manipulations of it by a member state must be consented to by the Fund or the member will lose its membership rights in respect to the Fund's operations. This arrangement is intended to curtail the type of harmful practices which occurred in the 1930's when states attempted to gain an economic advantage through unilateral devaluation.

INTERNATIONAL REFUGEE ORGANIZATION

The International Refugee Organization was established in 1946 by the General Assembly as a temporary, specialized agency of the United Nations, after a recommendation to establish such an agency by the Economic and Social Council. IRO took over from UNRRA, which was abolished in December of 1946, the problem of alleviating the plight of World War II refugees. Until its demise in January, 1952, IRO processed over a million refugees and its functions included camp maintenance, the supply of food and medical equipment, training and orientation, transportation, facilitation of repatriation, tracing services (to reunite families), and foster home placement. Most of those resettled were accepted by the United States, Australia, and New Zealand. Communist countries were opposed to the basic principles guiding IRO, particularly IRO's inclusion of "enemy" persons as refugees, and the practice of allowing refugees the right to refuse repatriation. For these and other reasons, UN communist states voted against the establishment of IRO and the major participants and contributors to IRO were non-communist states —i.e., Australia, Belgium, Canada, China, France, Italy, Norway, and the United States. Policy for IRO was established by a General Council (all member states) and carried out by a Director-General and Executive Committee (nine states). Contributions and expenditures to IRO exceeded 400 million dollars, roughly half of which was used for transportation to receiving states. IRO was headquarters in Geneva.

INTERNATIONAL TELECOMMUNICATION UNION (ITU)

The International Telecommunication Union, formed by the International Telecommunication Convention, coming into force in 1934, replaced the International Telegraph Union, formed by the Paris Convention of 1865. The Telecommunication Convention was drastically revised in 1947 at which time the ITU became a specialized agency of the United Nations. The structural innovations of the 1947 revisions became effective January 1, 1949. Additional revisions were made after the Buenos Aires Plenipotentiary Conference of 1952, the Geneva Conference of 1959, and the Montreux Conference of 1965. The latter revisions became effective January 1, 1967.

The organization's major purpose is to foster the rational use of telecommunications media and to promote state cooperation on such matters. To further these objectives, the Union: (1) makes studies and disseminates information; (2) provides training and technical assistance; (3) registers frequencies for individual stations to foster maximum rational use; and (4) allocates frequencies in respect to categories of use—such as maritime, meteorological, and coastal.

The principal organs of ITU are the Plenipotentiary Conference, the Administrative Conferences, the Administrative Council, the International Frequency Registration Board, the Consultative Committees, and the Secretary-General (Secretariat). The permanent headquarters are in Geneva, Switzerland. The Union publishes numerous materials, many of a highly technical nature such as lists of telephone routes and circuits, as well as a less technical monthly journal.

ITU

Administrative Conferences

Administrative Conferences deal with a particular communications area, particularly to consider revisions of the regulations which are annexed to the Telecommunication Convention. Two Conferences in which all members participate, one dealing with telegraph and telephone matters and the other with radio, normally meet close to the time of the Plenipotentiary Conference. The members of the Radio Conference supervise the work of the International Frequency Registration Board.

Administrative Council

The Administrative Council consists of twenty-nine members elected by the Plenipotentiary Conference to act on its behalf between conference meetings. The Council normally meets once a year and supervises the activities of the Secretary-General, the International Frequency Registration Board, and the Consultative Committees. The Council approves the annual budget in terms of guidelines laid down by the Plenipotentiary Conference and reports to the Conference.

Consultative Committees

Two Consultative Committees—specifically, the International Telegraphic and Telephone Consultative Committee and the International Radio Consultative Committee—study problems of a technical nature connected with tariffs, operations, safety, transmission, and circuitry. Members of interested international organizations and private organizations are members of these committees as well as representatives of states. Much of the work is accomplished through study groups which report to the Plenary Sessions of the committees, which normally meet every three years. The reports from the basis of technical recommendations made to members in the hope of fostering cooperation and the rational utilization of facilities.

Financing

The annual budget, set recently at $4,946,667, is borne by the ITU members who contribute in varying amounts in terms of a voluntary classification scheme which sets the amount of contribution. Generally speaking, the large states pay considerably less, as a fraction of total assessments, than in the case of the other specialized agencies.

International Frequency Registration Board

The five members of the International Frequency Board are elected by the Administrative Radio Conference, as technical experts with the primary function of recording broadcasting frequency usages. Also, the members provide technical advice, disseminate information, and may make certain types of investigations concerning the use of frequencies. The primary objective of the Board is to maximize the utilization of the broadcasting frequency spectrum.

Members

Membership is open to those entities specified in its convention. By February, 1967, there were 129 members. Interestingly, some entities which are not states, such as the Holy See and the French Overseas Territories, are accepted as full members. Virtually all states are members, including communist ones, with the exception of North Korea, North Vietnam, and Communist China.

Plenipotentiary Conference

All members may participate in the Plenipotentiary Conference, but only full members are entitled to vote. The Plenipotentiary Conference meets irregularly but meets at least once every five years. It determines the general policy of the organization, receives and considers the report of the Administrative Council, elects the members of the Administrative Council and the Secretary-General, adopts revisions to the Telecommunications Convention, and sets the upward limit on the expenses of the Organization.

Secretary-General

The Secretary-General, elected by the Plenipotentiary Conference, heads a Secretariat of over 430 persons in Geneva. The responsibilities of the Secretariat include those of servicing the other organs of the Union, making liaison and meeting arrangements, and disseminating information.

NON-SELF-GOVERNING TERRITORIES

The Charter of the United Nations, under Chapter XI, assumes responsibility for and imposes obligations on responsible states in respect to non-self-governing territories. Non-self-governing territories are defined as "territories whose peoples have not yet attained a full measure of self-government" (Article 73). Although this definition appears very broad, in practice, a number of entities which are not states nor clearly independent escape the classification of and provisions pertaining to non-self-governing territories. First, trust territories, because of Charter provisions elsewhere, are exempted from the reporting provision of Chapter XI. Second, "overseas territories", that is, non-contiguous entities considered parts of states, are exempted entirely from Chapter XI. The overseas territory of New Caledonia, as part of France, falls in this category. Finally, "self-governing" entities which are not states, such as Puerto Rico, are also exempted from Chapter XI. An important question arises, however, as to who decides upon these exemptions— the United Nations or individual states? Although the United Nations has repeatedly attempted to make such determinations, in practice, individual states may appear to decide in the final analysis. For example, Portugal has refused to report under Chapter XI and refused to take her alloted seat on the General Assembly's Committee on Information from Non-Self-Governing Territories, on the grounds that her overseas possessions are an integral part of Portugal. On occasion, the General Assembly has shifted a non-independent territory from the "non-self-governing" to "self-governing" classification. This was the case with Puerto Rico, after her "commonwealth" status was approved in 1952. This determination, in effect, ended United States responsibilities under Chapter XI of the Charter. (Puerto Ricans are United States citizens, subject to the draft, and appeals may be made from Puerto Rican courts to United States courts. Also, the United States is responsible for the defense and foreign affairs of Puerto Rico.) Non-self-governing matters are presently the responsibility of the Committee of Twenty-four, created in 1962 by the Assembly to oversee the application of the Declaration in the Granting of Independence to Colonial Countries and Peoples. The later declaration—along with one contained in the Charter, i.e., the "Declaration Regarding Non-Self-Governing Territories"—establishes the guidelines to be followed by responsible states toward such territories.

OBSERVATION GROUP (UNOGIL)

The United Nations Observation Group was formed by the Security Council in 1958, during the Lebanon crisis, for the purposes of observing the Lebanese borders to detect the passage of illegal personnel or arms into Lebanon. The Secretary-General was authorized to compose the force and did so out of the United Nations Truce Supervisory Organization located in Jerusalem. The peak strength of the group amounted to approximately 600 persons. The mission lasted from June-December 1958, during which time conditions sufficiently improved to terminate it.

OBSERVATION MISSION (UNYOM)

The United Nations Observation Mission in Yemen was created by the Security Council in 1963 to observe and report on the situation in Yemen in view of possible armed conflict between the United Arab Republic and Saudi Arabia. These states have actively supported opposite sides since the overthrow of the Yemen monarchy. After protracted conflict, a settlement between the parties was reached in August, 1965. In spite of this, however, tension and hostilities have continued.

OPERATION DES NATIONS UNIES AU CONGO (ONUC)

ONUC was formed following a request of Secretary General Hammarskjöld to the Security Council, on July 13, 1960. The chaotic situation in the Republic of the Congo was brought to the attention of the Secretary General after Congolese independence was granted, on June 30, 1960. The Security Council supported the Secretary General's request, on July 14, and gave him a mandate to compose a force to support the Congolese government. The Security Council resolution also requested that Belgium remove her troops from the Congo.

Within a few days Secretary General Hammarskjöld dispatched the initial contingent of approximately 3500 men. Moise Tshombe, President of Katanga, however, refused to allow the entry of ONUC into Katanga Province and, although Belgium removed her troops from the other portions of the Congo, they remained in Katanga. On August 8, the Security

Council authorized the Secretary General to have ONUC enter Katanga in order to implement the original resolution. The purpose of the mission was to take up areas of control vacated by Belgium troops. The Soviet Union, however, called for complete suppression of Tshombe by UN forces and this demand was also made by Patrice Lumumba, the Premier of the Central Government. Disputes over this matter, and others, led to a deadlock in the Security Council. The matter was turned over to the General Assembly in September, upon the initiative of the United States, using the Uniting for Peace Resolution.

In the meantime, the governmental situation in the Congo had become fragmented and disorganized. The General Assembly, in spite of USSR disapproval, supported the Secretary General's policies in respect to the Congo and his decisions concerning the application of force. When competing delegations from the Congo arrived, to be seated in the General Assembly, one headed by Congo President Kasavubu and the other by Lumumba, the Kasavubu delegation was seated. This further alienated the Soviet Union and certain other states from the Congo operation. Attacks by the Soviet Union were further intensified after the assassination of Lumumba in February, 1961. On February 21, 1961, the Security Council again considered the matter and authorized the Secretary General to take any measures necessary to prevent a civil war in the Congo and called for the withdrawal of Belgium and other foreign military troops. ONUC gradually grew to 23,000 men and intensive fighting developed between ONUC and the Katanga forces. After negotiations between the two sides, a cease fire was arranged, on September 21, 1961, and it was agreed that foreign troops were to be removed from Katanga. The Security Council further strengthened the Secretary General's hand, on November 13, when it authorized him to use forceful means if necessary to remove foreign military troops and the Council declared its support for the Congo Central Government. Fighting resumed, however, between ONUC and Katanga forces. Finally, in December, Tshombe decided, in view of defeats, to promise cooperation in the formation of a new government. Sporadic fighting continued, however, until January, 1963, after which Tshombe sought asylum in Spain. After completing pacification, ONUC forces were gradually reduced until June 30, 1964, when they were withdrawn.

Although ONUC was successful in its general mission of preventing fragmentation of the Congo, nevertheless, the operation was a costly one. The United Nations became deeply involved in a situation which alienated a number of states and which accentuated the financial crisis connected with peace-keeping operations.

ORIGINAL MEMBERS

Original members are United Nations members which ratified the United Nations Charter after signing the United Nations Declaration and/or after participating in the San Francisco Conference. (Poland is the only original member which did not participate in the Conference.) Other states are designated as subsequent members and must meet Charter qualifications and be brought in through certain procedures. The original members are: Argentina, Australia, Belgium, Bolivia, Brazil, Byelorussian S.S.R., Canada, Chile, China, Colombia, Costa Rica, Cuba, Czechoslovakia, Denmark, Dominican Republic, Ecuador, El Salvador, Ethiopia, France, Greece, Guatemala, Haiti, Honduras, India, Iran, Iraq, Lebanon, Liberia, Luxembourg, Mexico, Netherlands, New Zealand, Nicaragua, Norway, Panama, Paraguay, Peru, Philippines, Poland, Saudi Arabia, Turkey, Ukrainian S.S.R., Union of South Africa, Egypt (United Arab Republic), Union of Soviet Socialist Republics, United Kingdom, United States, Uruguay, Venezuela, and Yugoslavia.

Four of the above—India, Philippines, Ukrainian S.S.R.,

and Byelorussian S.S.R.—were not states when they became members, although India and the Philippines have since become states. This is true despite the Charter which maintains "The original Members . . . shall be the states" (Chapter II, Article 3). Technically, only forty-nine of the original members are presently states while two of them are sub-divisions of one state—the USSR. This stands in contrast to the legal status of subsequent members, all of which have been and presently are states.

PEACE-KEEPING FORCE IN CYPRUS (UNFICYP)

In February, 1964, the Security Council recommended that the General Assembly constitute a peace-keeping force for Cyprus, in view of fighting between Greek and Turkish Cypriots and the possibility of an armed clash between Greece and Turkey over the matter. The basic purpose of the force has been to pacify the situation by standing between the fighting groups. The force was expanded to approximately 6,000 by June, 1964. Since then, the United Nations has attempted numerous techniques to attempt to bring the two sides together and has repeatedly extended the life of UNIFCYP over its initial three-months duration.

PREPARATORY COMMISSION

The Preparatory Commission was a body created at the San Francisco Conference, in June, 1945, to make arrangements for the first meetings of the United Nations' principal organs. It was composed of all of the original signers of the Charter but much of the work was accomplished by an Executive Committee consisting of the USSR, United States, Great Britain, China, France, Canada, Czechoslovakia,

Chile, Brazil, Australia, Iran, Yugoslavia, Netherlands, and Mexico. The Executive Committee submitted a report to the full Commission in November, 1945. After study, revision, and acceptance by the Committee the report became recommendations to the major UN organs during their first meetings in 1946. Many of the present rules of procedure, with slight revision, are a result of this early work of the Preparatory Commission.

PRINCIPAL ORGANS

Article 7 of the Charter of the United Nations establishes the General Assembly, Security Council, Economic and Social Council, Trusteeship Council, International Court of Justice, and Secretariat as principal organs. All other organs are designated as specialized or subsidiary, and such distinctions are important for the operations and powers of the organs. In terms of actual relationships, however, the Security Council, General Assembly, and International Court of Justice may be viewed as relatively autonomous co-equals, while the Economic and Social Council and Trusteeship Council operate, basically, under the General Assembly. The Secretariat combines the characteristics of partial autonomy and partial subservience relative to the other principal organs.

PROVISION OF OPERATIONAL, EXECUTIVE, AND ADMINISTRATIVE PERSONNEL (OPEX)

The Opex Program was initiated by the General Assembly in 1958 and made operational in 1959. The Program provides technical assistance to states by arranging for the appointment of United Nations specialized agency officials to the governments desiring them. Such officials play an advisory role and help train state nationals to play the same role when the appointment period is over. Salaries are paid for by the recipient government and supplemented by the United Nations.

RECOMMENDATION

A recommendation, which can be contrasted with a decision, is the equivalent of a suggestion and, therefore, technically, has no legal consequences. This is not to say that recommendations may not have considerable political significance. Nevertheless, a state does not violate international law when it refuses to honor a UN recommendation. All UN organs other than the Security Council and International Court of Justice are limited to making recommendations.

SCALE OF ASSESSMENTS

The scale of assessments refers to the listed percentage contribution of the United Nations budget owed by member states as determined by the General Assembly, upon the recommendation of the Committee on Contributions. For example, in respect to the current scale, the United States is responsible for 31.91 per cent of the budget, the USSR 14.92 per cent, the United Kingdom 7.21 per cent, and so forth. The percentage is based on ability to pay calculated, basically, from information concerning national and per capita income. An important question arose after special assessments were levied to pay for General Assembly peace-keeping operations in the Suez and Congo crises as to whether member states are obligated to pay these costs, as they are in the case of regular assessments. The International Court of Justice was asked to give an advisory opinion on the subject in 1961 and the Court replied (July, 1962), in effect, that special assessments for peace-keeping operations by the General Assembly were to be paid by member states like regular assessments. Several states have ignored the advice of the Court on this matter, however. The General Assembly attempted to alleviate its financial situation by voting in 1961 to sell $200,000,000 worth of twenty-five year bonds to member states. Presumably, the bonds were to be paid off through regular assessments. A number of states, however, have refused to pay that portion of their assessments which were to be used to retire the bonds (i.e., USSR, France). Recently, various efforts have been made to solicit funds on a purely voluntary basis to take care of financial obligations not met by regular assessments. The budget for the 1967 financial year is $130,314,230, of which $72,751,830 is for staff costs and related expenses. (30, 239, 243)

SECRETARIAT

According to Article 97 of the Charter, "the Secretariat shall comprise a Secretary-General and such staff that the organization may require." The Secretary-General is designated as the "Chief administrative officer of the organization", and in this capacity he exercises a variety of powers and engages in numerous functions. All of the staff of the Secretariat, for example, are appointed by the Secretary-General in accordance, however, with the regulations established by the General Assembly. Dismissal of staff members, within the structures of the existing regulations, is also the prerogative of the Secretary-General. The Secretary-General sits in on meetings of the General Assembly, the Security Council, the Economic and Social Council, the Trusteeship Council, and other bodies and renders advice and performs functions which may be assigned to him. For example, he was given responsibility during the Suez crisis for composing the United Nations' Emergency Force and with a group of advisory states of directing it. The Secretary-General has also tried taking the initiative in efforts to mediate disputes, as in the Cuban missile crisis. His concern for political matters is clearly articulated in the Charter where he is given the right to "bring to the attention of the Security Council any matter which in his opinion may threaten the maintenance of international peace and security" (Article 99).

One of the primary functions of the Secretary-General is to direct the Secretariat—which collectively assists other organs; arranges for meetings; provides translation and documents; renders expert advice and assistance; and maintains the library services of the United Nations, constituting approximately 11,000 books, 300,000 periodicals and documents, and 3,000 maps. During the period from June, 1965, to May, 1966, for example, the Secretariat arranged over 2,322 meetings at United Nations' headquarters and over 2,000 meetings in Geneva.

Members of the Secretariat are recruited from member states applying the highest standards of efficiency, competency, and integrity with due regard being paid to geographical distribution. In regard to this latter criterion, of late, because of the General Assembly's policy guidelines which have pointed out maldistribution in respect to the Secretariat's staff, candidates are first considered from those states which have no nationals presently in the Secretariat. Secondly, they are recruited from those states in "under-represented regions," designated as Africa and Eastern Europe; and, thirdly, they are recruited from those states in "over-represented regions", i.e., Western Europe. Once employed, staff members are expected to give their primary loyalty to the United Nations and may not seek or receive instructions from any government or authority external to the United Nations. Also, each member state of the United Nations promises to "respect the exclusively international character of the responsibilities of the Secretary-General and the staff and not to seek to influence them in the discharge of their responsibilities" (Article 100, paragraph 2).

136

Presently—in order to maximize efficiency, continuity, and experience—fixed-term appointments, compared to career appointments, are held to approximately twenty-five percent of the total appointments.

The composition of the Secretariat as of May, 1966, consisted of 9,122 members. Only 6,147 of these, however, are regular members in posts provided for by the budget with the remaining 2,975 members performing functions in connection with United Nations subsidiary organs, paid for by voluntary contributions. 3,919 of the regular staff are located at United Nations' headquarters. 997 are at the European office in Geneva. The remainder are scattered out in the economic commissions for various regions, information centers, and in certain, special missions. 5,273 members of the total staff fall in the "field service", "general service," or "manual worker" category while 3,849 fall in the "professional or higher" category. (9, 28, 86, 103, 149, 277)

SECRETARIAT

Administrative Tribunal

The Administrative Tribunal, consisting of seven persons appointed by the General Assembly for three-year terms, hears cases relating to the terms of employment (dismissal, etc.) of the staff of the Secretariat and the staff of those specialized agencies which have made arrangements for its use through their agreements with the United Nations. Decisions of the Tribunal may be "appealed" only in the sense that the General Assembly may ask the International Court of Justice for an advisory opinion in respect to a case.

SECRETARIAT

Commissioner for Technical Assistance

The Commissioner for Technical Assistance, with the rank of Under-Secretary, heads the Bureau of Technical

Assistance Operations (BTAO) as part of the Department of Economic and Social Affairs. Prior to 1958 the Bureau was "independent" and known as the Technical Assistance Administration. The Bureau administers and provides facilities and services for technical assistance programs. It has worked closely with the Technical Assistance Board.

Controller

The Controller, who holds the rank of Under-Secretary, heads the Office of the Controller, supervises the treasury of the United Nations, including the collection of assessments and contributions of the members, and directs budgetary services. The Controller is immediately under the direction of the Secretary-General.

Department of Conference Services

The Department of Conference Services, headed by an Under-Secretary, makes arrangements for the meetings of the organs and conferences of the United Nations, other than the specialized agencies and certain other bodies, and prepares and issues publications and records. Also, it maintains the library of the United Nations.

Department of Economic and Social Affairs

The Department of Economic and Social Affairs, headed by an Under-Secretary, services all organs and activities dealing with economic and social affairs of the United Nations— particularly the Economic and Social Council, including its functional and regional economic commissions; and the

Economic and Financial Committee and the Social, Humanitarian, and Cultural Committee of the General Assembly. The Department also maintains liaison with the specialized agencies, although they possess their own secretariats.

Department of Political and Security Council Affairs

The Department of Political and Security Council Affairs, headed by an Under-Secretary, services the Security Council and its organs, the committees and organs of the General Assembly dealing with "political" matters (i.e., the Political and Security Committee), and the Disarmament Commission. It prepares various papers and studies needed by the above bodies and frequently renders technical advice.

Department of Trusteeship and Non-Self-Governing Territories

This department, headed by an Under-Secretary, is primarily concerned with servicing the Trusteeship Council, the Trusteeship Committee (Fourth), and the Committee of Twenty-four of the General Assembly. Various kinds of information are acquired and analyzed on behalf of the above organs in respect to their functions. The Trusteeship division of the Department, for example, aids the Trusteeship Council by considering petitions and annual reports by the Administering Authorities.

Director of Personnel

The Director of Personnel, who holds the rank of Under-Secretary, heads the Office of Personnel; administers the staffing of the Secretariat, including the training and recruitment of personnel; and operates directly under the Secretary-General.

Field Service

The Field Service was established in 1949 by a General Assembly resolution and is empowered to service (transportation, etc.) and make secure United Nations field operations. The service is uniformed, carries side arms in certain dangerous situations, operates under the Office of General Services, and is limited to a maximum of 300 men. Although Trygve Lie originally wanted a force with greater police powers, such as sufficient to supervise truces, the Service was limited to its, basically, service role by the General Assembly.

"Great Powers"

The permanent members of the Security Council have always received certain key positions in the Secretariat, in part, through gentlemen's agreements. Although the actual positions and their functions have changed over time, the concept of great power presence has persisted. Presently, persons from "great powers" hold, in fact, the following key positions: China (Taiwan), the Commissioner for Technical Assistance; the USSR, the Under-Secretary for Political and Security Council Affairs; the United Kingdom, the Director of Personnel and the Coadministrator of the UN Development Programme; France, the Under-Secretary for Economic and Social Affairs; and the United States, the Director of General Services, the Executive Director of the United Nations' Children's Fund, the Administrator of the UN Development Programme, and the Under-Secretary for Special Political Affairs.

Joint Advisory Committee

The Joint Advisory Committee, selected by the Staff Council and the Secretary-General, gives advice to the Secretary-General in respect to staff policy matters. This body along with the Joint Disciplinary Committee, Joint Appeals Board, Staff Council, and Administrative Tribunal, provides a buffer against purely arbitrary action by the Secretary-General regarding staffing matters.

Joint Appeals Board

The Joint Appeals Board, selected by the Secretary-General and Staff Council, advises the Secretary-General concerning complaints against administrative decisions.

Joint Disciplinary Committee

The Joint Disciplinary Committee, selected by the Staff Council and the Secretary-General, advises the Secretary-General regarding staff disciplinary matters.

Legal Counsel

The Legal Counsel, who holds the rank of Under-Secretary, heads the Office of Legal Affairs. His function is to advise and represent the Secretary-General on legal matters and render legal service to all other United Nations organs. The Legal Counsel is immediately under the direction of the Secretary-General.

Office of General Services

The Office of General Services, headed by an Under-Secretary, handles United Nations purchases, transportation, communication needs, building management, and security and field services.

Office of Public Information

The Office of Public Information, headed by an Under-Secretary, handles information dissemination, including press releases concerning the United Nations, and manages the various United Nations Information Centers in a number of states.

Secretary-General (Appointment)

The Secretary-General is appointed by the General Assembly (simple majority) upon the recommendations of the Security Council (veto applies). Because each permanent member of the Security Council possesses a veto over the recommendation, these members normally meet and agree on a candidate before full Council consideration. Under existing rules a deadlock between the Council and the Assembly is possible if the Assembly continually rejects the person recommended by the Council. In that the Charter is silent on the question of the length of term for the Secretary-General, the Assembly established a five-year term by resolution in 1946, with possible immediate reelection. After Trygve Lie's first term expired in February, 1951, the Assembly, on its own, extended his term for three additional years, in view of the Council's inability to recommend a candidate to the Assembly. The Council was deadlocked on the matter, because the USSR had vetoed Lie's renomination, basically, because of his support of the United Nations' action in the Korean Crisis and the United States announced that it would veto any other candidate. The USSR viewed the Assembly's decision to extend Lie's term as illegal and refused to recognize him as Secretary-General. The supporters of the Assembly's action pointed out that the Assembly had originally set the five-year term and, thus, presumably, the Assembly could change it. Difficulties concerning the Secretary-General arose again during Dag Hammarskjöld's active role in the Congo Crisis.

Staff Council

The Staff Council, elected by members of the Secretariat from the Secretariat, recommends improvements in work and life conditions of Secretarial staff members. It also participates with the Secretary-General in the selection of the Joint Disciplinary Committee, Joint Appeals Board, and Joint Advisory Committee.

"Troika" Plan

The "troika" plan refers to the proposal of the USSR that the Secretary-General's office should be replaced with a three-man directorate (each man with a veto) reflecting the three "forces" of the modern world—that is, the Western, "socialist" (i.e. communist), and the neutralist states. The proposal was precipitated by the USSR's dissatisfaction with the role of Dag Hammarskjöld in the Congo crisis. Basically, the USSR charged that Hammarskjöld was acting partially and was favoring the Western states. Various secretariat modifications were also suggested by certain "neutralist" states at the time. The death of Hammarskjöld, on September 17, 1961, and the election of U Thant ended consideration of the "troika" proposal, which never received more than minimal support, especially, in view of Hammarskjöld's opposition to it.

SECURITY COUNCIL

The Security Council is designated as a principal organ, by Article 7 of the Charter, and specializes in problems involving the maintenance of peace and security, operating primarily under Chapters 6 and 7.

The Security Council embodies the principle that the "big five" are primarily responsible for peace and security but allows this function to be shared with the non-permanent members of the Council. In the League of Nations system the Assembly and the Council were more or less co-partners in respect to problems of peace and security. (Although, initially, there was great power dominance on the Council.) In the United Nations system, on the other hand, the Charter makes a fairly clear division of labor between the organs, and the Security Council stands out as the *primary* organ of peace-keeping (although the General Assembly is not prohibited from dealing with matters of aggression.) This shift in emphasis between the two systems may be characterized as a movement away from the Wilsonian concept of the "all against the few" to a new concept emphasizing great power perquisites and responsibilities for the collective security system.

Because it is primarily an organ of emergency, the Security Council is required, by Article 28, to be organized so that it can function continuously. This stands in contrast to the General Assembly's temporary existence during its sessions. (However, the advantage of the Security Council's "permanent session" has been undercut somewhat by the fact that the General Assembly now can come into special, emergency session, within a twenty-four hour period, under the Uniting For Peace Resolution.)

Members of the United Nations "confer on the Security Council primary responsibility for the maintenance of international peace and security, and agree that in carrying out its duties and under this responsibility the Security Council acts on their behalf" (Charter, Article 24). Further, they "agree to accept and carry out the decisions of the Security Council in accordance with the present Charter" (Charter, Article 25). These commitments stand in contrast to members' rights, under the League of Nations, to decide for themselves whether the covenant had been violated.

The fundamental assumption behind the successful operation of the Security Council is "great power harmony," in that each of its permanent members possess a veto. The failure to obtain great power harmony in the post-war world helps explain the relative eclipse of the Security Council through most of its existence, in comparison with the General Assembly. The most notable shift in the direction of augmenting the General Assembly's responsibilities, in the supposed area of "primary concern" of the Security Council, occurred during the Korean War with the General Assembly's adoption of the Uniting for Peace Resolution.

SECURITY COUNCIL

Credentials

The Secretary-General reviews the credentials of representatives to the Security Council and the Security Council decides credential matters. Although the Secretariat examines the credentials of representatives to the General Assembly and reports to the Credentials Committee, because each organ decides credential matters for itself, there exists the possibility of a discrepancy concerning credentials between the two organs. That is, the existing system makes it possible that the Security Council could accept the credentials of representatives who are not accepted by the General Assembly or vice versa.

Disarmament

The Security Council, under Article 26, is charged with "formulating, with the assistance of the Military Staff Committee . . . plans to be submitted to the Members of the United Nations for the establishment of a system for the regulation of armaments." The guiding principle in respect to these plans is, presumably, to maintain "international peace and security with the least diversion for armaments of the world's human and economic resources." Much of the Council's responsibility, in fact, has been taken over by subsidiary organs such as the Atomic Energy Commission, the Commission on Conventional Armaments, and the Disarmament Commission. Also, a considerable portion of negotiation concerning disarmament matters has gone on between the large nuclear powers, basically, outside of the United Nations. Thus, the Security Council and the Military Staff Committee have never really played the major role concerning disarmament apparently envisioned by the framers of the organization.

Dispute

A dispute refers to an international development where parties are in disagreement and which can possibly endanger the maintenance of international peace and security. The Security Council can investigate a dispute to see if it "is likely to endanger the maintenance of peace and security"

(Article 34). If a dispute is deemed not likely to endanger peace and security the Security Council may make recommendations with a view to pacific settlement only if the parties so request. If the dispute is deemed likely to endanger peace and security the Council may "call upon" the parties to use peaceful settlement methods (Article 33, 2); "recommend" specific methods (Article 36, 1); or, if the parties bring the dispute to the Security Council after their failure to achieve a settlement by pacific means, "recommend such terms of settlement as it may consider appropriate" (Article 37, 2). Permanent members of the Security Council who are parties to a dispute must abstain from voting when the Council is operating under Chapter VI. A permanent member may use its veto, however, to prevent the Council from considering a matter a dispute. Disputes may be brought to the attention of the Security Council or General Assembly by any members of the United Nations and by any non-member who is a party to a dispute that accepts "the obligations of pacific settlement provided for in the present Charter" (Article 35, 3).

SECURITY COUNCIL
"Double Veto"

The term "double veto," which does not appear in the Charter, refers, by popular usage, to the right of a permanent member to challenge the President of the Security Council in respect to his ruling as to whether a matter is procedural or substantive and then through the use of the veto make the matter substantive so that the veto applies in decisions.

SECURITY COUNCIL
"Invited Members"

The Security Council can invite members of the United Nations to participate in Security Council discussions without a vote if it considers such members' interests especially affected (Article 31). Non-members of the Organization which are parties to a dispute may also be invited to participate without a vote under conditions established by the Security Council. For example, Communist China was invited to participate in Security Council discussions early in the Korean War.

Military Staff Committee

The Military Staff Committee, composed of the Chiefs of Staff of the permanent members of the Security Council or their representatives, was to: (1) advise the Security Council on force agreements and requirements to maintain peace and security; (2) give strategic direction, under the Security Council, for armed forces at the disposal of the Security Council; and (3) advise and assist the Security Council in respect to the regulation of armaments (Article 26, **47**). The Military Staff Committee first met, in February, 1946, and shortly thereafter considered, upon the Security Council's request, the problem of bringing forces under the Security Council as provided for in Article 43. The Committee's report of April, 1947, revealed disagreements between the major powers, especially between the US and the USSR, particularly on the questions of: (1) the size of the forces, (2) the location of the forces when not used by the Security Council, (3) the balance of the forces, and (4) arrangements concerning use of bases and facilities. In general, the USSR wanted smaller, balanced forces (each member to contribute the same force components) stationed when not in use in the donating country; while, the United States preferred larger forces composed of what each member was best able to contribute stationed to the best advantage of the Security Council even when not in use. Although agreement was reached upon a number of other points (twenty-five in all) the above contentious points and certain others led the Committee to report, in July, 1948, that further progress was not possible. Since then, the Committee has been basically non-functional, with its armament regulation functions absorbed by various commissions and its strategic, direction functions provided on an *ad hoc* basis when United Nations forces are employed, as in the Korean crisis.

Non-Permanent Members

The non-permanent members of the Security Council are elected for two-year terms (staggered) by the General Assembly (two-thirds majority required) with the Assembly presumably guided "in the first instance to the contribution of Members . . . to the maintenance of international peace and security and to the other purposes of the Organization, and also to equitable geographic distribution" (Article 23). In practice, seats are allocated primarily in terms of group-geographic factors (i.e., Latin American group) with little regard for the potential contribution of candidate states to the maintenance of peace and security. Until the end of 1965 there were six non-permanent seats. Since then, the number has been raised to ten through amendment of the Charter. Non-permanent members are not eligible for immediate re-election. The major distinction, besides seat retention, between permanent and non-permanent members lies in the veto power of the former.

Permanent Members

The permanent members of the Security Council are named in the Charter as "The Republic of China, France, the Union of Soviet Socialist Republics, the United Kingdom of Great Britain and Northern Ireland, and the United States of America" (Article 23 (1)). Because the permanent members

149

are named in this fashion, a Charter amendment is necessary to alter the arrangement. Thus, over time, a discrepancy could conceivably occur between the power status of those named members and the "power reality" within the international system, unless redressed by amendment. Permanent members originally obtained their status because of their "great power" position in the post-World War II world. In addition to their perpetual seat on the Council, permanent members possess the veto power over substantive questions and Charter amendments, with the qualification that a party to a dispute must abstain from voting in decisions under Chapter VI. Permanent members also hold automatic representation on the Military Staff Committee. Otherwise, permanent members have the same privileges as non-permanent members.

President

The President of the Security Council is its principal officer, who exercises powers similar to those of the President of the General Assembly. Presidents of the Council are not elected; rather, each member of the Council holds the Presidency for one month, with the possession of the office rotating according to alphabetical order. The President of the Council may call meetings on his own initiative and also does so upon the request of a member of the Security Council or the Secretary-General or when a dispute is called to the attention of the Council by the General Assembly or a member state.

Procedural Questions

A procedural question is one where the veto power of the permanent members of the Council does not normally apply. This includes such questions as the creation of subsidiary organs, the adoption of new rules of procedure, the bringing in of "invited members," the place of meetings, and the passing of a question to the General Assembly. There is some ambiguity on these matters, however, in that, at times, questions that have been considered procedural have been made substantive through the exercise of the double veto. Agenda items themselves, however, are always considered procedural. General Assembly efforts to have the permanent members of the Security Council extend the list of questions considered procedural, to reduce the scope of the veto, have been unsuccessful.

SECURITY COUNCIL

Situation

The term "situation" refers to an international development that can lead to "international friction", a "dispute", or "endanger the maintenance of international peace and security" (Charter, Article 34). The Security Council is authorized to investigate all such situations to determine whether the provisions of Chapter VI are applicable. In practice, there seems to be little distinction between the use of the terms "situation" and "dispute" by the Council, although the former term does seem to have somewhat broader connotations. If a determination concerning a situation does lead to the application of Chapter VI a permanent member involved in the situation retains its veto power, in contrast to a dispute in which it is involved. If a situation is ascertained as likely to endanger the maintenance of international peace and security the Council may "recommend appropriate procedures or methods of adjustment" (Article 33, 1). Any member of the United Nations can bring a situation to the attention of either the Security Council or the General Assembly.

Substantive Question

A substantive question is one where the veto power of the permanent members of the Council may be exercised. This includes all important questions such as Charter amendments; a determination of a dispute or situation in respect to Chapter VI or Chapter VII; the application of sanctions; the recommendation of the appointment of the Secretary-General; and the admission, suspension, or expulsion of members. If there is a question as to whether a matter is substantive or procedural the veto applies in the sense that it can make the matter substantive, with the exception that certain matters are normally understood to be procedural and the question of agenda composition is always considered procedural.

Veto

Although the term "veto" does not appear in the Charter, in general usage it applies to the right of a permanent member of the Security Council to prevent a Security Council decision on substantive questions by a negative vote. The Charter provides "Decisions of the Security Council on all other matters [other than procedural] shall be made by an affirmative vote of nine [previously seven] members including the concurring votes of the permanent members" (Article 27 (3)). This passage seems to imply that each of the permanent members must favor (cast a positive vote) a decision or it is vetoed. In practice, however, neither physical absence from the Council, as that of the USSR at the beginning of the Korean War, or abstention have been viewed by the Council as constituting a veto. In the Korean example, on the other hand, the USSR did protest that her absence and other factors made the Security Council decisions, at that time, illegal. The use of the veto power is qualified by the provision that "in decisions under Chapter VI, and under paragraph 3 of Article 52, a party to a dispute shall abstain from voting" (Article 27 (3)). Chapter VI refers to the use of regional arrangements to facilitate pacific settlement. Presumably then, each of the permanent members may lose its veto power if it is a party to a dispute and the Security Council is relying upon the above articles in its decisions. It is possible, however, for a permanent member to use its veto to prevent a Security Council determination that a conflict is a "dispute" and, therefore, retain its veto power in any attempted decisions on such matters. All of the permanent members with the exception of the United States have used their veto power, although the vast majority of vetoes have been cast by the USSR. (146, 151, 261)

SECURITY COUNCIL

Voting

Each member of the Security Council, whether permanent or non-permanent, has one vote. Nine or more affirmative votes decide procedural and substantive matters, with the qualification in respect to substantive matters that no permanent member cast a negative vote, and that a party to a dispute shall not vote. These rules make the veto applicable to most Security Council decisions, although elections to the International Court of Justice only require a "veto free" absolute majority decision. These rules are a reflection of the supposed need to obtain "great power harmony" on most important Security Council matters.

SINGLE CONVENTION ON NARCOTIC DRUGS

The Single Convention on Narcotic Drugs was adopted by a special conference held for that purpose at the United

Nations in January-March, 1961. It has entered into force, after ratification by forty states, and by June, 1966 fifty-three states were signatories. The Single Convention coalesces previous treaties in the narcotics area and establishes a tighter system of control. Under the convention an eleven-man International Narcotics Control Board, to become functional on March 2, 1968, will absorb the powers and functions of the Central Opium Board and the Drug Supervisory Body. The election of the Control Board was arranged for by the Secretary-General of the United Nations, in 1967, at the request of the Economic and Social Council.

SPECIAL COMMITTEE
(COMMITTEE OF TWENTY-FOUR)

The Special Committee was created, in 1961, by the General Assembly to facilitate the implementation of the Assembly's Declaration on the Granting of Independence to Colonial Countries and Peoples. The Committee initially had seventeen members but was enlarged to its present size of twenty-four in 1962. The Committee's members reflect a geographic balance and are nominated by the President of the General Assembly. In 1963, the functions of the Committee on Information for Non-Self-Governing Territories were turned over to the Special Committee.

SPECIAL FUND

The Special Fund was created, on January 1, 1959, by a resolution of the General Assembly. Its purpose is to stimulate the economic development of less developed countries by investing and facilitating investments in important projects. The Fund operates in what might be referred to as preinvestment areas in partnership with recipient governments. Primarily, then, it stimulates further investment by investing in survey training, education, and research projects. Much is accomplished in cooperation with and through other international agencies, such as the International Labor Organization and the Food and Agricultural Organization. Projects are financed through voluntary contributions raised through pledging conferences. Structurally, the Fund has been administered by a Managing Director who has made recommendations in respect to projects, which have been reviewed by consultative boards and approved by an eighteen-member Governing Council. The Council has been elected by the Economic and Social Council and has been divided between economically "advanced" and "developing" states.

In August, 1964, the Economic and Social Council recommended a consolidation (completed January 1, 1966) of the Special Fund with the Expanded Program of Technical Assistance, creating a new "United Nations Development Programme." Although the separate missions and financing of the Fund and Expanded Program remain, an Inter-Agency Consultative Board replaces both the Technical Assistance Board of the Expanded Program and the Consultative Board of the Fund, and a Governing Council replaces the Technical Assistance Committee of the Expanded Program and the Governing Council of the Fund.

Recently, the Special Fund had approved assistance for 604 large-scale projects expected to cost $1,406,000,000 upon completion. Of this amount, $823,000,000 will be contributed by recipient governments.

"SUBSEQUENT MEMBERS"

All members of the United Nations which are not original members may be classified as "subsequent members." Article 4 of the Charter opens the organization to "all other peace-loving states which accept the obligations contained in the present Charter and in the judgment of the Organization are able and willing to carry out these obligations." Procedurally, the Security Council recommends (veto applies) and the General Assembly decides (two-thirds majority) upon membership. Conflicts in the Security Council in the post-war period between East and West over their respective "candidates" i.e., Italy (West), Bulgaria (East) lead to a partial deadlock in the Security Council over admissions, preventing the Security Council from making recommendations to the General Assembly concerning membership for a number of states. It became clear that criteria other than those specified in the Charter were being applied in some cases. After a request from the General Assembly, the International Court of Justice gave an advisory opinion on the subject in 1948, maintaining, in effect, that only the Charter criteria should apply and that it would be improper to make approval of one state contingent upon the approval of another state. Thus, presumbly, each state was to be admitted on its own merits if it met Charter requirements. Regardless of this opinion, however, the deadlock persisted. In view of this, the General Assembly asked the Court whether it would be proper for the General Assembly to admit states on its own. The Court replied, in effect, in an advisory opinion in 1950, that the Security Council recommendation was an essential prerequisite in the admissions process. The deadlock over admissions was broken in 1955 when the Security Council recommended to admit sixteen states, after a bargain to link the admission together, despite the earlier Court opinion. Since that time virtually all states wishing to gain admission have been able to do so. Certain important entities, however, do remain outside the organization. These are: Switzerland, German Federal Republic (West), German Democratic Republic (East), Republic of Korea (South), Democratic People's Republic of Korea (North), Republic of Vietnam (South), and Democratic Republic of

Vietnam (North). All except Switzerland, whose non-membership is an expression of her "neutrality", have partially clouded legal existences relating to partition which are basically a product of the cold war.

SUSPENSION

A Member of the United Nations may have its rights of membership suspended by the General Assembly (two-thirds vote) upon the recommendation of the Security Council (veto applies). Presumably, suspension is evoked only when "preventive or enforcement action has been taken by the Security Council" (Article 5). Restoration of suspended rights is determined by the Security Council alone. Thus far, no state has had its rights of membership suspended.

TEN-NATION COMMITTEE
ON DISARMAMENT

The General Assembly created the Ten-Nation Committee on Disarmament, in 1959, as a supplement to the Disarmament Commission, in an effort to continue progress on disarmament problems. Unlike the Disarmament Commission, membership of the Ten-Nation Committee was divided equally between East and West. Shortly thereafter, however, the Assembly modified the composition by enlarging the committee to eighteen members which brought in a number of neutral states.

TRANSITIONAL SECURITY
ARRANGEMENTS

Article 106 of the Charter empowers the permanent members of the Security Council to "consult with one another as occasion requires with other Members of the United Nations with a view to such joint action on behalf of the Organization as may be necessary for the purpose of maintaining international peace and security." However, this privilege is qualified by the proviso that it may be exercised "pending the coming into force of such special agreements referred to in Article 43" (Article 43 concerns the placing of national military contingents under the Security Council). Because the provisions of Article 43 have never come into effect, from a purely technical point of view, the permanent members of the Council can presumably still rely on Article 106. However, it has never been used, and perhaps it would be best to consider it to have become defunct from lack of use. In any case, this article cannot be considered to allow the unilateral action by one of the permanent members because it only authorizes "joint action on behalf of the organization."

Another transitional matter is treated in Article 107 which provides "nothing in the present Charter shall invalidate or preclude action, in relation to any state which during the Second World War has been an enemy of any signatory to the present Charter, taken or authorized as a result of that war by the Governments having responsibility for such action." Presumably, although not clearly, these provisions cease to apply when an enemy state regains its status as an ordinary member of the international community through a peace treaty. At present, then, this article seems to apply only to Germany. In that no final peace treaty has been signed concerning Germany, can several states including the USSR and the United States take action against Germany without violating the Charter? From one perspective, it would seem that such action is "legally" possible. However, it is apparent that time has eroded the readiness of states to accept the implications of this Article. On the other hand, during the Berlin Crisis of 1948 the Soviet Union maintained that action could be taken by the USSR in regard to her occupation zone in Germany without it becoming a concern of the United Nations. Also, the Warsaw Pact, directed against Western Germany, is based, in part, upon Article 107. Article 107 is tied to Article 53 which provides:

> no enforcement action shall be taken under regional arrangements or by regional agencies without the authorization of the Security Council, with the exception of measures against any enemy state . . . provided for pursuant to Article 107 or in regional arrangements directed against renewal of aggressive policy on the part of any such state, until such time as the Organization may, on request of the Governments concerned, be charged with the responsibility for preventing further aggression by such a state.

In that the USSR has never requested that the Organization take responsibility in respect to Germany, from the USSR's perspective, possible Warsaw Pact action against Germany-Western is excepted from the above requirement of Security Council authorization.

TREATY REGISTRATION

Article 102 of the Charter provides that all treaties and international agreements entered into after the signing of the Charter must be "as soon as possible registered with the Secretariat and published by it." This provision, found also in the Covenant, reflects the Wilsonian idea that all treaties and agreements should be "open" to prevent the kind of secret diplomatic bargains that occurred before and during World War I. In the Charter, a sanction is provided to encourage compliance with this provision, in that any agreements or treaties which are not registered cannot be invoked "before any organ of the United Nations." Thus, an unregistered treaty can not be cited in a case before the International Court of Justice nor in connection with decisions of the Security Council. This does not prevent other non-United

Nations tribunals, however, from considering such treaties as a component of international law. In this respect, the Charter provisions differ markedly from those of the Covenant in that, in the case of the latter unregistered treaties were not "binding until so registered" (Covenant, Article 18). At present, in spite of these provisions, states do frequently engage in agreements that are not registered with the Secretariat and, therefore, not published. Many of these concern the alliances of East and West. Exact state responsibilities in the event of a conflict as to who will do what, when, and where, are, of course, presently tantamount to "military secrets," and, in spite of the fact that they are international agreements, are not registered with the Secretariat. It is apparent, then, that the sanction provided for is not a sufficient inducement to overcome the apparent sense of security derived from keeping these agreements unregistered in violation of the Charter. On the other hand, states do adhere to the letter of the Charter in respect to the more general alliance commitments they have undertaken (i.e., the texts of the NATO Treaty and the Warsaw Pact Treaty are duly registered).

TRUSTEESHIP COUNCIL

The Trusteeship Council is designated as a principal organ of the United Nations by Article 7 of the UN Charter, and it has special responsibilities for the international trusteeship system, provided for by Chapter 12. The objectives of the trusteeship system, according to Article 76 of the Charter, are:

to further international peace and security; . . . to promote the political, economic, social, and educational advancement of the inhabitants of the trust territories, and their progressive development towards self-government or independence as may be appropriate to the particular circumstances of each territory and its people and the freely expressed wishes of the peoples concerned, and as may be provided by the terms of each trusteeship agreement; . . . to encourage respect for human rights and for fundamental freedoms for all without distinction as to race, sex, language, or religion, and to encourage recognition of the interdependence of the peoples of the world; and . . . to insure equal treatment in social, economic, and commercial matters for all members of the United Nations and their nationals and also equal treatment for the latter in the administration of justice, without prejudice to the attainment of the foregoing objectives . . .

The Trusteeship Council, like the Economic and Social Council, operates under the authority of the General Assembly which reviews its work and approves the trusteeship agreements. The Trusteeship Council has diminished in size as trust territories have become independent and will disappear entirely when all such areas have attained their independence. (66, 95, 249)

TRUSTEESHIP COUNCIL

Administering Authority

The Administering Authority is the state (or states) responsible, through agreements approved by the General Assembly (or the Security Council in the case of strategic areas), for the development of trust territories in the Trusteeship System. The part played by the Administering Authority is an outgrowth of the role of the Mandatory in the League of Nations mandates system. The original Administering Authorities were Australia, Belgium, France, Italy, New Zealand, United Kingdom, and the United States (some with more than one trust territory). All but the United States and Italy had been mandatories in the League system.

Meetings

Two sessions of the Council, starting in January and June, were held each year until 1963. Since then, one session has been held in May. Special sessions may be held upon the request of the Security Council, the General Assembly, a majority of members of the Trusteeship Council, or by a decision of the Trusteeship Council.

Members of

The Trusteeship Council consists of administering authorities, "permanent members" who are also permanent members of the Security Council, and enough elected members (three-year terms) so that the Council membership is balanced between trust and non-trust states. Until 1960 the Council had fourteen members. Since that time, the size has decreased as the majority of the trust territories have been independent or parts of other independent states. Presently there is one elected state, one "non-permanent" administering authority (Australia), two "permanent" administering authorities (United Kingdom and the United States), and three "permanent" non-administering states (China, France, and the USSR).

Oral Hearing

The Council may grant oral hearings upon request, usually in connection with a petition. Such oral hearings were granted, for example, in connection with the granting of independence to the Cameroons, Togoland, and Tanganyika.

Questionnaire

The Council is authorized, by Article 88 of the Charter, to prepare a questionnaire to be completed by the Administering Authority, to be used by the Council in its annual reports. The questionnaire is complex and probing, covering, in detail, political, economic, social, educational, and security questions as well as other matters. Each report is formally examined by the Council, leading to a general discussion. The usual procedure is to have an opening statement by a representative of the Administering Authority to the Council and then an exchange of written and oral questions and answers between the Authority and members of the Council. Information gathered in this way—along with other data from visiting missions, petitions, and other possible sources, such as the specialized agencies—allows the Council to come to conclusions and make recommendations.

Reports

The Council makes reports to the Security Council for strategic areas and to the General Assembly for all other trust territories. Reports are based on petitions, oral hearings, questionnaires, visiting missions, and other possible sources of information. Reports describe conditions, summarize discussions, and list recommendations for each territory. Possible recommendations to Administering Authorities by the Security Council and the General Assembly are based on these reports. In the case of the General Assembly, the Fourth Committee (Trusteeship) uses reports and additional information, such as gathered through oral hearings, to make recommendations to the plenary session of the Assembly.

Standing Committee on Petitions

The device of a Standing Committee on Petitions was employed from 1952 to 1962. It was created each session to screen the flow of petitions from the trust territories. The members of the Committee were divided equally between Council members from administering the non-administering states. The Administering Authority concerned had the right to explain and present views to the Committee, regarding the petitions, prior to the Committee's report to the Council. Since 1962, petition functions have been taken over by the Council itself.

Trusteeship Agreements

Trusteeship agreements specify the terms under which trust territories are administered by administering authorities. They are negotiated by the Trusteeship Council with administering authorities and approved by the Security Council in the case of strategic trust areas, and by the General Assembly for all other territories.

Visiting Missions

The Council has the right, under Article 87 of the Charter, to "provide for periodic visits to the respective trust territories at times agreed upon with the administering authority." In practice, each of the territories has been visited approximately once every three years, although special missions may be sent at more frequent intervals. The mission normally consists of four members, two of which are derived from states named by the Administering Authority and two of which come from other states. The information gathered by the mission, on a wide variety of subjects, may be used in the Council's report to the General Assembly and to advise the Administering Authority.

Voting

Each member of the Council possesses one vote and decisions are made by a majority of members present and voting (Article 89). Although the permanent members of the Security Council are always present on the Council they possess no special voting privileges.

TRUSTEESHIP SYSTEM

Maintenance of Peace and Security

Article 84 of the Charter provides:

> It shall be the duty of the administering authority to ensure that the trust territory shall play its part in the maintenance of international peace and security. To this end the administering authority may make use of volunteer forces, facilities, and assistance from the trust territory in carrying out the obligations towards the Security Council undertaken in this regard by the administering authority, as well as for local defense and the maintenance of law and order within the trust territory.

This provision reverses the role of such territories in the League of Nations system in that mandatories were instructed to prevent "the establishment of fortification or military and naval bases and of military training of the natives for other than police purposes and the defense of the territory" (Covenant, Article 22, 5). Although the administering authority can not employ conscription it can establish bases and utilize and, as indicated above, use "volunteer forces" for collective security action as well as local defense and order.

Petitions

Any person has the right to petition the Trusteeship Council regarding conditions in the trust territories with the qualification that petitions should not concern disputes which the courts of the Administering Authority can deal with and should not be directed against court judgments. Court judgments, however, must be based on laws that are consistent with the United Nations Charter and trusteeship agreements. Petitions can be sent to the Secretary-General, the Administering Authority, or presented to members of visiting missions dispatched by the Council. The Council considers petitions and may make resolutions concerning them to Administering Authorities. Thousands of petitions, covering a wide variety of matters, have been received and considered in the operation of the Trusteeship system.

Strategic Areas

The strategic areas are part or all of trust territories designated as such in trusteeship agreements. The only trust territories so designated are the Pacific Islands (Marshalls, Carolines, and Marianas, excepting Guam) with the United States as administering authority. These areas were previously Japanese mandates under the League mandates system. The major difference between strategic areas and non-strategic areas (all others) is that in the case of the former: (1) the Security Council approves (veto applies) the trusteeship agreement, (2) the basic objectives of the trusteeship system are qualified by security considerations, and (3) the Trusteeship Council's supervision powers are less than in the case of non-strategic areas.

Trust Territories

Trust territories are areas under the supervision of an administering authority in the Trusteeship System. Three types of areas were originally contemplated as subject to the status of trust territories: (1) mandates under the League of Nations, (2) detached territories (from every state) as the result of World War II, and (3) territories voluntarily placed under the system (such as colonies). The original trust territories were New Guinea, Nauru (Australia); Ruanda-Urundi (Belgium); Cameroons, Togoland (France); Cameroons, Togoland, Tanganyika (United Kingdom); Pacific Islands (United States); Western Samoa (New Zealand); and Somaliland (Italy). All but Somaliland, a former Italian colony detached because of World War II, were League mandates. No additional territories have been voluntarily placed under the system. Presently, only New Guinea and the Pacific Islands remain as trust territories. The rest have become independent or are part of independent states.

UNITED NATIONS EMERGENCY FORCE

The United Nations Emergency Force was established, by a General Assembly resolution of November 5, 1956, to supervise the cessation of hostilities extending from the Suez Canal to armistice demarcation lines established between Egypt and Israel. The creation of the force followed an Israeli invasion of the Sinai Peninsula of Egypt on October 29, 1956, and subsequent French and British military action against Egypt. After consideration and deadlock in the Security Council concerning the Suez situation the matter passed by the Uniting for Peace Resolution to the General Assembly, and the Secretary-General was requested to draw plans for a supervisory force. After a plan was adopted, the force was constituted and became operational, on November 15, 1956. The Secretary-General and a seven-nation advisory committee were given primary responsibility for directing the force, which quickly grew to approximately six thousand men at a cost of about $40,000 per day. Ten states—Brazil, Canada, Colombia, Denmark, Finland, India, Indonesia, Norway, Sweden, and Yugoslavia—supplied military contingents while a number of other states assisted by supplying medical equipment, food and other materials. Although the General Assembly attempted to finance a sizeable portion of the operation by applying the scale used in connection with regular assessments certain states have objected and have refused to pay any assessments connected with the Emergency Force. Although the functions of the force have continued, it has been reduced in size, in part because of the financial crisis engendered by its existence. (84, 85, 143, 200, 218)

UNIVERSAL POSTAL UNION (UPU)

In 1874, the first International Postal Congress, meeting in Bern, Switzerland, established, through the International Postal Convention, the General Postal Union. The second congress, held in 1878, renamed the organization the Universal Postal Union. Various postal congresses, held prior to World War II, extended and amended the Convention. In 1947, the Postal Congress held in Paris amended the Convention to make UPU a specialized agency of the United Nations, upon agreement of the General Assembly. Subsequent postal congresses have further altered the Convention with the provisions adopted at the Vienna Congress, of 1964, presently effective.

The basic purpose of the Union is to perfect postal services within the area embraced by the Union and to promote international cooperation in respect to such services. To further these objectives the Union: engages in research; provides technical assistance; arbitrates disputes between member states, concerning regulations; and facilitates the settling of financial accounts generated by international postal services.

The principal organs are: the Universal Postal Congress, the Executive and Liaison Committee, the Consultative Commission on Postal Studies, and the Secretary-General (International Bureau).

The organization is responsible for numerous publications such as the *Abridged Postal Statistics* and the *Compendium of Internal Postal Charges and Internal Services of Administrations* and a monthly journal entitled *Postal Union.*

UPU

Congress

The Congress consists of all UPU members, each entitled to one vote. It has as its primary function the review and modification of the Universal Postal Convention. The entire territory of the member states is viewed as a "single territory" to which the Convention applies for all ordinary mail, such as letters, postcards, commercial papers, etc. All members are bound to apply the uniform standards established by the Convention within the territory. Other services —such as C. O. D., money orders, insured letters, and parcel post—are covered by special agreements which bind only those members which adhere to them. In addition to work on the Convention, the Congress elects the Executive and

Liaison Committee and reviews the functions of the organization. Although the Congress meets irregularly, it must meet at least once every five years.

UPU

Consultative Committee for Postal Studies

The Consultative Committee for Postal Studies was created by the Ottawa Conference of 1957 for the purpose of carrying out studies and rendering technical advice on various aspects of postal service. Each member of UPU is a member of the Committee, although a twenty-six member Management Council coordinates and directs the work. In 1966, the Council undertook studies of mechanization and automation of accounting, technological advances in postal services of developing countries, and methods of reaching staff requirements in post offices.

UPU

Director (International Bureau)

The Director of the International Bureau is appointed by the Executive and Liaison Committee and heads a small staff (approximately) at the headquarters in Bern. The Bureau is responsible for: liaison work with member states and other organizations; information gathering and dissemination; various service arrangements; and facilitates the settling of accounts between states in respect to their postal services.

UPU

Executive Council

The Executive Council (before 1965, the Executive and Liaison Committee) consists of twenty-seven members elected by the Congress according to the formula of: five for the Americans; five for Western Europe; three for Eastern Europe and North Asia; seven for Southeast Europe, South Asia, and Oceania; and seven for Africa. The Council provides continuity between Congresses. In this capacity, it supervises the work of the International Bureau and appoints its Director, maintains relationships with other international organizations, makes studies, and provides technical information to members. It also reviews possible revisions in the Postal Convention and makes recommendations to the Congress.

UPU

Financing

Member states meet ordinary, annual expenses through a contributions classification scheme ranging from one to seven, whereby the lower the class the higher the assessment due. The classification of a particular member is determined by the Swiss government in agreement with the government concerned. For example, Canada, France, India, New Zealand, United Kingdom, and the United States fell into class one, while the Ivory Coast, Iceland, and Mali fall into class seven. Maximum, annual expenditures are established by each Congress. A recent budget was set at $1,405,000. Income from the sale of documents and certain other sources also helps defray expenses.

UPU

Members

Prior to 1947, any state wishing to become a member of the Union could do so by accession to the Universal Postal Convention. Since that time, new applicants after notifying the Swiss government must be approved by a two-thirds absolute majority of UPU members. The Union embraces most states, including communist ones, as members. The

Union does not include, however, North Vietnam, North Korea, or Communist China. On June 5, 1964, South Africa was expelled from UPU by the UPU Congress. South Africa's expulsion was controversial because it related to the practice of *apartheid* rather than the violation of UPU regulations.

UPU
Training Committee

In 1964, an eight nation Training Committee was established by the UPU Congress to make recommendations regarding postal training needs. In 1965, the Committee approved a plan to create a "UPU Special Fund" for training activities. The plan has been accepted by the Executive Council and is financed by voluntary contributions.

WITHDRAWAL

The Charter of the United Nations does not mention the question of or procedures for withdrawal from the organization. It is generally assumed that each state has the exclusive right to make such a determination. Indonesia is the only state to have exercised this right (January, 1965) and did so in the face of requests not to do so, including that of the Secretary-General. In September 1966, Indonesia rejoined the organization.

WORLD FOOD PROGRAM (WFP)

The World Food Program, initiated by the Food and Agricultural Organization and the United Nations in 1961, with a $100 million pledge target, consists of an effort to utilize voluntary contributions of money, services, and food to counteract local food emergency situations; create national food reserves; facilitate school and pre-school nutrition; and aid in food development projects. A twenty-four nation committee, twelve of which are elected by FAO and twelve by the Economic and Social Council of the United Nations, directs the program. After an initial three-year experimental period, the program has continued with a virtual trebling of scope. Forty-five countries have pledged over $205 million dollars of food, money, and services toward the $275 million target of the 1966–68 program ($130 million has been pledged by the United States).

WORLD HEALTH ORGANIZATION (WHO)

The World Health Organization came into legal existence on April 7, 1948, after twenty-six states had ratified its constitution and became functional on September 1 of the same year. WHO's constitution was formulated and adopted by the International Health Conference of June-July, 1946, sponsored by the Economic and Social Council of the United Nations. WHO absorbed the assets and functions of the League Health Organization and the International Office of Public Health and transformed some regional sanitary bureaus, possessing prior, separate existences, into regional offices. The Organization's basic purpose is to promote the highest possible level of health by coordinating international health work, conducting and promoting research, gathering and disseminating information, providing technical assistance and services, establishing and promoting standardization procedures and nomenclature, and proposing agreements and conventions on international health matters. The principal organs to accomplish these objectives and functions are the World Health Assembly, the Executive Board, and the Director (Secretariat). The permanent headquarters are in Geneva, Switzerland, but much of the work is done in the regional offices. The Organization is responsible for a large number of diverse materials including: *Bulletin of the World Health Organization, Chronicle of World Health Organization, World Health,* and *Weekly Epidemiological Record.*

Assembly

The World Health Assembly, which meets annually, normally in Geneva, consists of delegates from member states with each member possessing one vote. The Assembly establishes the basic policy and programs of the organization, approves the budget, appoints the Director-General, elects the Executive Board, and adopts, by a two-thirds vote, conventions and regulations. Conventions if accepted through proper constitutional procedures by member states become binding upon the signatories. Each state is obligated to submit Assembly adopted conventions to its constitutional processes within eighteen months of adoption. State ratifying organs concerned, however, are not under more than a moral obligation to ratify the conventions. Regulations adopted by the Assembly are binding on all states except those who object to the regulations within a certain time period. It is normal to consider a particular health problem of world wide importance at each annual conference.

Director-General (Secretariat)

The Director-General, appointed by the Assembly, heads the Secretariat composed of a technical and administrative staff of more than 3,190 persons. A sizeable portion of the work at the central headquarters in Geneva consists of coordinating the very active, regional offices. In fact, over two-thirds of the staff working on behalf of WHO are located somewhere other than at the central headquarters. The members of the Secretariat engage in a wide variety of functions including technical assistance, information collection and dissemination, and various services.

Executive Board

The Executive Board consists of twenty-four qualified individuals, designated by member states elected by the World Health Assembly, following the rule of equitable geographic distribution. Persons so designated operate in terms of the dictates of their technical competence rather than as delegates of the appointing state. The Board normally meets twice a year but may hold special sessions. The primary function of the Board is to supervise the execution of the policies decided upon by the Assembly. Also, it is authorized to take certain emergency measures in unusual circumstances, acting through the Director-General and his Secretariat.

Financing

WHO finances its various functions through voluntary contributions, participation in the United Nations Development Programme, and a regular budget. Each member pays a portion of the regular budget according to a scale of contributions. For example, the United States' share is approximately thirty percent, the Soviet Union's share approximately fourteen percent, and the United Kingdom's share approximately seven percent. A recent budget was set at $57,935,000.

Membership

Members of the United Nations may become members of WHO by accepting the WHO constitution and giving notification of this fact to the Secretary-General of the United Nations. States that are not members of the United Nations may be admitted, after application, upon acceptance by the World Health Assembly (majority vote). Certain entities that are not full states may be admitted by the Assembly as associate members. By February, 1967, the Organization had 124 full members, including the communist states of the United Nations, and three associate members.

WORLD METEOROLOGICAL ORGANIZATION (WMO)

WMO came into formal existence in March, 1950, after thirty states had ratified the World Meteorological Convention which had been adopted by a Conference of Directors of national meteorological services held in Washington, D.C. in 1947. WMO was preceded by the International Meteorological Organization (IMO), created in 1878 by a conference held at Utrecht, Netherlands, IMO consisted of an association of the directors of national meteorological services and was not viewed as constituting an inter-governmental organization until 1939 when states, rather than directors, became members. After the acceptance of the 1947 WMO Convention, the functions and assets of IMO were absorbed by WMO and the latter became a specialized agency of the United Nations, reporting to the Economic and Social Council. The basic purposes of WMO are to promote: the establishment of meteorological stations and centers; the creation of systems of weather information exchange; standardization of procedures and nomenclature; the application of weather information to the various human activities such as aviation and shipping; and further research and training activities connected with meteorology. In addition, WMO may make recommendations to states, propose conventions, and perform research and technical assistance functions. The principal organs are the Congress, the Executive Committee, and the Secretary-General (Secretariat). WMO is responsible for a variety of technical publications including a quarterly *WMO Bulletin*. The permanent headquarters are in Geneva, Switzerland.

Congress

The WMO Congress is the primary policy-making body of the organization, consisting of delegates (directors of meteorological services) of members. Each member possesses one vote, with a simple majority deciding elections and a two-thirds majority of those voting deciding other questions. An important function of the Congress is the adoption of technical regulations pertaining to meteorological practices. In addition, the Congress elects the President, two Vice-Presidents, and members of the Executive Committee. The World Meteorological Convention requires that the Assembly meet at least once every four years.

Executive Committee

The Executive Committee consists of twenty-one directors of national meteorological services and automatically includes WMO's President, the two Vice-Presidents and the presidents of the Regional Associations. The remaining members are elected by the Congress. The Committee makes decisions by a two-thirds majority vote and operates, basically, to carry out policies determined by the WMO Congress. It also engages in studies, advises members, and makes recommendations to the Congress.

177

Financing

A regular four-year budget is approved by the WMO Congress and is paid by the members according to a scale of assessments established by the Congress. The scale of assessments reflects ability to pay, with the United States paying the highest portion, the USSR the second highest portion, the United Kingdom the third highest portion, and so forth. The 1967 budget amounts to $2,433,960. WMO also receives monies as a participant in the United Nations Development Programme and acts as an executing agency for meteorological projects connected with the United Nations Special Fund.

Members

Applicants (not necessarily states) which maintain separate meteorological services are potential members of WMO. Entities which attended the 1947 WMO conference and members of the United Nations can become members of WMO simply by adhering to the WMO Convention. Other entities may become members, upon application, if approved by two-thirds of the members of the organization. By February, 1967, the bulk (129) of the world's potentially acceptable applicants had become members, including many communist states. The communist states of China, North Vietnam, and North Korea, however, are not members.

Regional Associations

Regional associations are organizations of the members of WMO drawing membership on a regional basis—i.e., Europe, North and Central America, South America, and the Southwest Pacific. Regional Associations meet when necessary and foster cooperation among their members, particularly in respect to information exchange and the maintenance of meteorological stations. They also perform functions based on the resolutions of the WMO Congress and examine, from a regional perspective, questions submitted to them by the Executive Committee. The president of each Regional Association is automatically a member of the Executive Committee.

Secretary-General (Secretariat)

The Secretary-General heads a small staff (180 in 1967) in Geneva and operates under the direction of the Executive Committee and the WMO Congress. The secretariat functions as a communications center, engages in technical studies, performs secretarial services for the other organs, and is responsible for publications.

Technical Commissions

The Congress of WMO has established eight technical commissions, composed of experts, to engage in technical studies of areas such as aeronautical meteorology, maritime meteorology, and agricultural meteorology. The commissions make recommendations, usually concerning procedures and technical regulations, to the Executive Committee and to the WMO Congress. The meetings of the Executive Committee and the Congress are attended by the officers of the commissions and they may participate but not vote in these bodies.

CHARTER OF THE UNITED NATIONS

WE THE PEOPLES OF THE UNITED NATIONS DETERMINED

to save succeeding generations from the scourge of war, which twice in our lifetime has brought untold sorrow to mankind, and to reaffirm faith in fundamental human rights, in the dignity and worth of the human person, in the equal rights of men and women and of nations large and small, and
to establish conditions under which justice and respect for the obligations arising from treaties and other sources of international law can be maintained, and to promote social progress and better standards of life in larger freedom,

AND FOR THESE ENDS

to practice tolerance and live together in peace with one another as good neighbors, and
to unite our strength to maintain international peace and security, and
to ensure, by the acceptance of principles and the institution of methods, that armed force shall not be used, save in the common interest, and
to employ international machinery for the promotion of the economic and social advancement of all peoples,

HAVE RESOLVED TO COMBINE OUR EFFORTS TO ACCOMPLISH THESE AIMS.

Accordingly, our respective Governments, through representatives assembled in the city of San Francisco, who have exhibited their full powers found to be in good and due form, have agreed to the present Charter of the United Nations and do hereby establish an international organization to be known as the United Nations.

CHAPTER I

Purposes and Principles

Article 1

The Purposes of the United Nations are:

1. To maintain international peace and security, and to that end: to take effective collective measures for the prevention and removal of threats to the peace, and for the suppression of acts of aggression or other breaches of the peace, and to bring about by peaceful means, and in conformity with the principles of justice and international law, adjustment or settlement of international disputes or situations which might lead to a breach of the peace;

2. To develop friendly relations among nations based on respect for the principle of equal rights and self-determination of peoples, and to take other appropriate measures to strengthen universal peace;

3. To achieve international cooperation in solving international problems of an economic, social, cultural, or humanitarian character, and in promoting and encouraging respect for human rights and for fundamental freedoms for all without distinction as to race, sex, language, or religion; and

4. To be a center for harmonizing the actions of nations in the attainment of these common ends.

Article 2

The Organization and its Members, in pursuit of the Purposes stated in Article 1 shall act in accordance with the following Principles.

1. The Organization is based on the principle of the sovereign equality of all its Members.

2. All Members, in order to ensure to all of them the rights and benefits resulting from membership, shall fulfil in good faith the obligations assumed by them in accordance with the present Charter.

3. All Members shall settle their international disputes by peaceful means in such a manner that international peace and security, and justice, are not endangered.

4. All Members shall refrain in their international relations from the threat or use of force against the territorial integrity or political independence of any state, or in any other manner inconsistent with the Purposes of the United Nations.

5. All Members shall give the United Nations every assistance in any action it takes in accordance with the present Charter, and shall refrain from giving assistance to any state against which the United Nations is taking preventive or enforcement action.

6. The Organization shall ensure that states which are not Members of the United Nations act in accordance with these Principles so far as may be necessary for the maintenance of international peace and security.

7. Nothing contained in the present Charter shall authorize the United Nations to intervene in matters which are essentially within the domestic jurisdiction of any state or shall require the Members to submit such matters to settlement under the present Charter; but this principle shall not prejudice the application of enforcement measures under Chapter VII.

CHAPTER II

Membership

Article 3

The original Members of the United Nations shall be the states which, having participated in the United Nations Conference on International Organization at San Francisco, or having previously signed the Declaration by United Nations of January 1, 1942, sign the present Charter and ratify it in accordance with Article 110.

Article 4

1. Membership in the United Nations is open to all other peace-loving states which accept the obligations contained in the present Charter and, in the judgment of the Organization, are able and willing to carry out these obligations.

2. The admission of any such state to membership in the United Nations will be effected by a decision of the General Assembly upon the recommendation of the Security Council.

Article 5

A Member of the United Nations against which preventive or enforcement action has been taken by the Security Council may be suspended from the exercise of the rights and privileges of membership by the General Assembly upon the recommendation of the Security Council. The exercise of these rights and privileges may be restored by the Security Council.

Article 6

A Member of the United Nations which has persistently violated the Principles contained in the present Charter may be expelled from the Organization by the General Assembly upon the recommendation of the Security Council.

CHAPTER III

Organs

Article 7

1. There are established as the principal organs of the United Nations: a General Assembly, a Security Council, an Economic and Social Council, a Trusteeship Council, an International Court of Justice, and a Secretariat.

2. Such subsidiary organs as may be found necessary may be established in accordance with the present Charter.

Article 8

The United Nations shall place no restrictions on the eligibility of men and women to participate in any capacity and under conditions of equality in its principal and subsidiary organs.

CHAPTER IV

The General Assembly

COMPOSITION

Article 9

1. The General Assembly shall consist of all the Members of the United Nations.

2. Each member shall have not more than five representatives in the General Assembly.

FUNCTIONS AND POWERS

Article 10

The General Assembly may discuss any questions or any matters within the scope of the present Charter or relating to the

183

powers and functions of any organs provided for in the present Charter, and, except as provided in Article 12, may make recommendations to the Members of the United Nations or to the Security Council or to both on any such questions or matters.

Article 11

1. The General Assembly may consider the general principles of cooperation in the maintenance of international peace and security, including the principles governing disarmament and the regulation of armaments, and may make recommendations with regard to such principles to the Members or to the Security Council or to both.

2. The General Assembly may discuss any questions relating to the maintenance of international peace and security brought before it by any Member of the United Nations, or by the Security Council, or by a state which is not a Member of the United Nations in accordance with Article 35, paragraph 2, and, except as provided in Article 12, may make recommendations with regard to any such questions to the state or states concerned or to the Security Council or to both. Any such question on which action is necessary shall be referred to the Security Council by the General Assembly either before or after discussion.

3. The General Assembly may call the attention of the Security Council to situations which are likely to endanger international peace and security.

4. The powers of the General Assembly set forth in this Article shall not limit the general scope of Article 10.

Article 12

1. While the Security Council is exercising in respect of any dispute or situation the functions assigned to it in the present Charter, the General Assembly shall not make any recommendations with regard to that dispute or situation unless the Security Council so requests.

2. The Secretary-General, with the consent of the Security Council, shall notify the General Assembly at each session of any matters relative to the maintenance of international peace and security which are being dealt with by the Security Council and shall similarly notify the General Assembly, or the Members of the United Nations if the General Assembly is not in session, immediately the Security Council ceases to deal with such matters.

1. The General Assembly shall initiate studies and make recommendations for the purpose of:

a. promoting international cooperation in the political field and encouraging the progressive development of international law and its codification;

b. promoting international cooperation in the economic, social, cultural, educational, and health fields, and assisting in the realization of human rights and fundamental freedoms for all without distinction as to race, sex, language, or religion.

2. The further responsibilities, functions, and powers of the General Assembly with respect to matters mentioned in paragraph 1 (b) above are set forth in Chapters IX and X.

Article 14

Subject to the provisions of Article 12, the General Assembly may recommend measures for the peaceful adjustment of any situation, regardless of origin, which it deems likely to impair the general welfare or friendly relations among nations, including situations resulting from a violation of the provisions of the present Charter setting forth the Purposes and Principles of the United Nations.

Article 15

1. The General Assembly shall receive and consider annual and special reports from the Security Council; these reports shall include an account of the measures that the Security Council has decided upon or taken to maintain international peace and security.

2. The General Assembly shall receive and consider reports from the other organs of the United Nations.

Article 16

The General Assembly shall perform such functions with respect to the international trusteeship system as are assigned to it under Chapters XII and XIII, including the approval of the trusteeship agreements for areas not designated as strategic.

Article 17

1. The General Assembly shall consider and approve the budget of the Organization.

2. The expenses of the Organization shall be borne by the Members as apportioned by the General Assembly.

3. The General Assembly shall consider and approve any financial and budgetary arrangements with specialized agencies referred to in Article 57 and shall examine the administrative budgets of such specialized agencies with a view to making recommendations to the agencies concerned.

VOTING

Article 18

1. Each member of the General Assembly shall have one vote.

2. Decisions of the General Assembly on important questions shall be made by a two-thirds majority of the members present and voting. These questions shall include: recommendations with respect to the maintenance of international peace and security, the election of the non-permanent members of the Security Council, the election of the members of the Economic and Social Council, the election of members of the Trusteeship Council in accordance with paragraph 1 (c) of Article 86, the admission of new Members to the United Nations, the suspension of the rights and privileges of membership, the expulsion of Members, questions relating to the operation of the trusteeship system, and budgetary questions.

3. Decisions on other questions, including the determination of additional categories of questions to be decided by a two-thirds majority, shall be made by a majority of the members present and voting.

Article 19

A Member of the United Nations which is in arrears in the payment of its financial contributions to the Organization shall have no vote in the General Assembly if the amount of its arrears equals or exceeds the amount of the contributions due from it for the preceding two full years. The General Assembly may, nevertheless, permit such a member to vote if it is satisfied that the failure to pay is due to conditions beyond the control of the Member.

PROCEDURE

Article 20

The General Assembly shall meet in regular annual sessions and in such special sessions as occasion may require. Special sessions shall be convoked by the Secretary-General at the request of the Security Council or of a majority of the Members of the United Nations.

The General Assembly shall adopt its own rules of procedure. It shall elect its President for each session.

The General Assembly may establish such subsidiary organs as it deems necessary for the performance of its functions.

CHAPTER V

The Security Council

COMPOSITION

Article 23

1. The Security Council shall consist of eleven Members of the United Nations. The Republic of China, France, the Union of Soviet Socialist Republics, the United Kingdom of Great Britain and Northern Ireland, and the United States of America shall be permanent members of the Security Council. The General Assembly shall elect six other Members of the United Nations to be non-permanent members of the Security Council, due regard being specially paid, in the first instance to the contribution of Members of the United Nations to the maintenance of international peace and security and to the other purposes of the Organization, and also to equitable geographical distribution.

2. The non-permanent members of the Security Council shall be elected for a term of two years. In the first election of the non-permanent members, however, three shall be chosen for a term of one year. A retiring member shall not be eligible for immediate re-election.

3. Each member of the Security Council shall have one representative.

FUNCTIONS AND POWERS

Article 24

1. In order to ensure prompt and effective action by the United Nations, its Members confer on the Security Council

187

primary responsibility for the maintenance of international peace and security, and agree that in carrying out its duties under this responsibility the Security Council acts on their behalf.

2. In discharging these duties the Security Council shall act in accordance with the Purposes and Principles of the United Nations. The specific powers granted to the Security Council for the discharge of these duties are laid down in Chapters VI, VII, VIII, and XII.

3. The Security Council shall submit annual and, when necessary, special reports to the General Assembly for its consideration.

Article 25

The Members of the United Nations agree to accept and carry out the decisions of the Security Council in accordance with the present Charter.

Article 26

In order to promote the establishment and maintenance of international peace and security with the least diversion for armaments of the world's human and economic resources, the Security Council shall be responsible for formulating, with the assistance of the Military Staff Committee referred to in Article 47, plans to be submitted to the Members of the United Nations for the establishment of a system for the regulation of armaments.

VOTING

Article 27

1. Each member of the Security Council shall have one vote.

2. Decisions of the Security Council on procedural matters shall be made by an affirmative vote of seven members.

3. Decisions of the Security Council on all other matters shall be made by an affirmative vote of seven members including the concurring votes of the permanent members; provided that, in decisions under Chapter VI, and under paragraph 3 of Article 52, a party to a dispute shall abstain from voting.

PROCEDURE

Article 28

1. The Security Council shall be so organized as to be able to function continuously. Each member of the Security Council

shall for this purpose be represented at all times at the seat of the Organization.

2. The Security Council shall hold periodic meetings at which each of its members may, if it so desires, be represented by a member of the government or by some other specially designated representative.

3. The Security Council may hold meetings at such places other than the seat of the Organization as in its judgment will best facilitate its work.

Article 29

The Security Council may establish such subsidiary organs as it deems necessary for the performance of its functions.

Article 30

The Security Council shall adopt its own rules of procedure, including the method of selecting its President.

Article 31

Any Member of the United Nations which is not a member of the Security Council may participate, without vote, in the discussion of any question brought before the Security Council whenever the latter considers that the interests of that Member are specially affected.

Article 32

Any Member of the United Nations which is not a member of the Security Council or any state which is not a Member of the United Nations, if it is a party to a dispute under consideration by the Security Council, shall be invited to partcipate, without vote, in the discussion relating to the dispute. The Security Council shall lay down such conditions as it deems just for the participation of a state which is not a Member of the United Nations.

CHAPTER VI

Pacific Settlement of Disputes

Article 33

1. The parties to any dispute, the continuance of which is likely to endanger the maintenance of international peace and

security, shall, first of all, seek a solution by negotiation, enquiry, mediation, conciliation, arbitration, judicial settlement, resort to regional agencies or arrangements, or other peaceful means of their own choice.

2. The Security Council shall, when it deems necessary, call upon the parties to settle their dispute by such means.

Article 34

The Security Council may investigate any dispute, or any situation which might lead to international friction or give rise to a dispute, in order to determine whether the continuance of the dispute or situation is likely to endanger the maintenance of international peace and security.

Article 35

1. Any Member of the United Nations may bring any dispute, or any situation of the nature referred to in Article 34, to the attention of the Security Council or of the General Assembly.

2. A state which is not a Member of the United Nations may bring to the attention of the Security Council or of the General Assembly any dispute to which it is a party if it accepts in advance, for the purposes of the dispute, the obligations of pacific settlement provided in the present Charter.

3. The proceedings of the General Assembly in respect of matters brought to its attention under this Article will be subject to the provisions of Articles 11 and 12.

Article 36

1. The Security Council may, at any stage of a dispute of the nature referred to in Article 33 or of a situation of like nature, recommend appropriate procedures or methods of adjustment.

2. The Security Council should take into consideration any procedures for the settlement of the dispute which have already been adopted by the parties.

3. In making recommendations under this Article the Security Council should also take into consideration that legal disputes should as a general rule be referred by the parties to the International Court of Justice in accordance with the provisions of the Statute of the Court.

1. Should the parties to a dispute of the nature referred to in Article 33 fail to settle it by the means indicated in that Article, they shall refer it to the Security Council.

2. If the Security Council deems that the continuance of the dispute is in fact likely to endanger the maintenance of international peace and security, it shall decide whether to take action under Article 36 or to recommend such terms of settlement as it may consider appropriate.

Without prejudice to the provisions of Articles 33 to 37, the Security Council may, if all the parties to any dispute so request, make recommendations to the parties with a view to a pacific settlement of the dispute.

CHAPTER VII

Action With Respect to Threats to the Peace, Breaches of the Peace, and Acts of Aggression

The Security Council shall determine the existence of any threat to the peace, breach of the peace, or act of aggression and shall make recommendations, or decide what measures shall be taken in accordance with Articles 41 and 42, to maintain or restore international peace and security.

In order to prevent an aggravation of the situation, the Security Council may, before making the recommendations or deciding upon the measures provided for in Article 39, call upon the parties concerned to comply with such provisional measures as it deems necessary or desirable. Such provisional measures shall be without prejudice to the rights, claims, or position of the parties concerned. The Security Council shall duly take account of failure to comply with such provisional measures.

The Security Council may decide what measures not involving the use of armed force are to be employed to give effect to its decisions, and it may call upon the Members of the United Nations to apply such measures. These may include complete or partial interruption of economic relations and of rail, sea, air, postal, telegraphic, radio, and other means of communication, and the severance of diplomatic relations.

Article 42

Should the Security Council consider that measures provided for in Article 41 would be inadequate or have proved to be inadequate, it may take such action by air, sea, or land forces as may be necessary to maintain or restore international peace and security. Such action may include demonstrations, blockade, and other operations by air, sea, or land forces of Members of the United Nations.

Article 43

1. All Members of the United Nations, in order to contribute to the maintenance of international peace and security, undertake to make available to the Security Council, on its call and in accordance with a special agreement or agreements, armed forces, assistance, and facilities, including rights of passage, necessary for the purpose of maintaining international peace and security.

2. Such agreement or agreements shall govern the numbers and types of forces, their degree of readiness and general location, and the nature of the facilities and assistance to be provided.

3. The agreement or agreements shall be negotiated as soon as possible on the initiative of the Security Council. They shall be concluded between the Security Council and Members or between the Security Council and groups of Members and shall be subject to ratification by the signatory states in accordance with their respective constitutional processes.

Article 44

When the Security Council has decided to use force it shall, before calling upon a Member not represented on it to provide armed forces in fulfillment of the obligations assumed under Article 43, invite that Member, if the Member so desires, to participate in the decisions of the Security Council concerning the employment of contingents of that Member's armed forces.

Article 45

In order to enable the United Nations to take urgent military measures, Members shall hold immediately available national air-force contingents for combined international enforcement action. The strength and degree of readiness of these contingents and plans for their combined action shall be determined, within the limits laid down in the special agreement or agreements referred to in Article 43, by the Security Council with the assistance of the Military Staff Committee.

Article 46

Plans for the application of armed force shall be made by the Security Council with the assistance of the Military Staff Committee.

Article 47

1. There shall be established a Military Staff Committee to advise and assist the Security Council on all questions relating to the Security Council's military requirements for the maintenance of international peace and security, the employment and command of forces placed at its disposal, the regulation of armaments, and possible disarmament.

2. The Military Staff Committee shall consist of the Chiefs of Staff of the permanent members of the Security Council or their representatives. Any Member of the United Nations not permanently represented on the Committee shall be invited by the Committee to be associated with it when the efficient discharge of the Committee's responsibilities requires the participation of that Member in its work.

3. The Military Staff Committee shall be responsible under the Security Council for the strategic direction of any armed forces placed at the disposal of the Security Council. Questions relating to the command of such forces shall be worked out subsequently.

4. The Military Staff Committee, with the authorization of the Security Council and after consultation with appropriate regional agencies, may establish regional subcommittees.

Article 48

1. The action required to carry out the decisions of the Security Council for the maintenance of international peace and

security shall be taken by all the Members of the United Nations or by some of them, as the Security Council may determine.

2. Such decisions shall be carried out by the Members of the United Nations directly and through their action in the appropriate international agencies of which they are members.

Article 49

The Members of the United Nations shall join in affording mutual assistance in carrying out the measures decided upon by the Security Council.

Article 50

If preventive or enforcement measures against any state are taken by the Security Council, any other state, whether a Member of the United Nations or not, which finds itself confronted with special economic problems arising from the carrying out of those measures shall have the right to consult the Security Council with regard to a solution of those problems.

Article 51

Nothing in the present Charter shall impair the inherent right of individual or collective self-defense if an armed attack occurs against a Member of the United Nations, until the Security Council has taken the measures necessary to maintain international peace and security. Measures taken by Members in the exercise of this right of self-defense shall be immediately reported to the Security Council and shall not in any way affect the authority and responsibility of the Security Council under the present Charter to take at any time such action as it deems necessary in order to maintain or restore international peace and security.

CHAPTER VIII

Regional Arrangements

Article 52

1. Nothing in the present Charter precludes the existence of regional arrangements or agencies for dealing with such matters relating to the maintenance of international peace and security as are appropriate for regional action, provided that such arrange-

ments or agencies and their activities are consistent with the Purposes and Principles of the United Nations.

2. The Members of the United Nations entering into such arrangements or constituting such agencies shall make every effort to achieve pacific settlement of local disputes through such regional arrangements or by such regional agencies before referring them to the Security Council.

3. The Security Council shall encourage the development of pacific settlement of local disputes through such regional arrangements or by such regional agencies either on the initiative of the states concerned or by reference from the Security Council.

4. This Article in no way impairs the application of Articles 34 and 35.

Article 53

1. The Security Council shall, where appropriate, utilize such regional arrangements or agencies for enforcement action under its authority. But no enforcement action shall be taken under regional arrangements or by regional agencies without the authorization of the Security Council, with the exception of measures against any enemy state, as defined in paragraph 2 of this Article, provided for pursuant to Article 107 or in regional arrangements directed against renewal of aggressive policy on the part of any such state, until such time as the Organization may, on request of the Governments concerned, be charged with the responsibility for preventing further aggression by such a state.

2. The term enemy state as used in paragraph 1 of this Article applies to any state which during the Second World War has been an enemy of any signatory of the present Charter.

Article 54

The Security Council shall at all times be kept fully informed of activities undertaken or in contemplation under regional arrangements or by regional agencies for the maintenance of international peace and security.

CHAPTER IX

International Economic and Social Cooperation

Article 55

With a view to the creation of conditions of stability and well-being which are necessary for peaceful and friendly relations among nations based on respect for the principle of equal rights and self-determination of peoples, the United Nations shall promote:

a. higher standards of living, full employment, and conditions of economic and social progress and development;

b. solutions of international economic, social, health, and related problems; and international cultural and educational cooperation; and

c. universal respect for, and observance of, human rights and fundamental freedoms for all without distinction as to race, sex, language, or religion.

Article 56

All Members pledge themselves to take joint and separate action in cooperation with the Organization for the achievement of the purposes set forth in Article 55.

Article 57

1. The various specialized agencies established by intergovernmental agreement and having wide international responsibilities, as defined in their basic instruments, in economic, social, cultural, educational, health, and related fields, shall be brought into relationship with the United Nations in accordance with the provisions of Article 63.

2. Such agencies thus brought into relationship with the United Nations are hereinafter referred to as specialized agencies.

Article 58

The Organization shall make recommendations for the coordination of the policies and activities of the specialized agencies.

Article 59

The Organization shall, where appropriate, initiate negotiations among the states concerned for the creation of any new specialized agencies required for the accomplishment of the purposes set forth in Article 55.

Article 60

Responsibility for the discharge of the functions of the Organization set forth in this Chapter shall be vested in the

General Assembly and, under the authority of the General Assembly, in the Economic and Social Council, which shall have for this purpose the powers set forth in Chapter X.

CHAPTER X

The Economic and Social Council

COMPOSITION

Article 61

1. The Economic and Social Council shall consist of eighteen Members of the United Nations elected by the General Assembly.

2. Subject to the provisions of paragraph 3, six members of the Economic and Social Council shall be elected each year for a term of three years. A retiring member shall be eligible for immediate re-election.

3. At the first election, eighteen members of the Economic and Social Council shall be chosen. The term of office of six members so chosen shall expire at the end of one year, and of six other members at the end of two years, in accordance with arrangements made by the General Assembly.

4. Each member of the Economic and Social Council shall have one representative.

FUNCTIONS AND POWERS

Article 62

1. The Economic and Social Council may make or initiate studies and reports with respect to international economic, social, cultural, educational, health, and related matters and may make recommendations with respect to any such matters to the General Assembly, to the Members of the United Nations, and to the specialized agencies concerned.

2. It may make recommendations for the purpose of promoting respect for, and observance of, human rights and fundamental freedoms for all.

3. It may prepare draft conventions for submission to the General Assembly, with respect to matters falling within its competence.

4. It may call, in accordance with the rules prescribed by

the United Nations, international conferences on matters falling within its competence.

Article 63

1. The Economic and Social Council may enter into agreements with any of the agencies referred to in Article 57, defining the terms on which the agency concerned shall be brought into relationship with the United Nations. Such agreements shall be subject to approval by the General Assembly.

2. It may coordinate the activities of the specialized agencies through consultation with and recommendations to such agencies and through recommendations to the General Assembly and to the Members of the United Nations.

Article 64

1. The Economic and Social Council may take appropriate steps to obtain regular reports from the specialized agencies. It may make arrangements with the Members of the United Nations and with the specialized agencies to obtain reports on the steps taken to give effect to its own recommendations and to recommendations on matters falling within its competence made by the General Assembly.

2. It may communicate its observations on these reports to the General Assembly.

Article 65

The Economic and Social Council may furnish information to the Security Council and shall assist the Security Council upon its request.

Article 66

1. The Economic and Social Council shall perform such functions as fall within its competence in connection with the carrying out of the recommendations of the General Assembly.

2. It may, with the approval of the General Assembly, perform services at the request of Members of the United Nations and at the request of specialized agencies.

3. It shall perform such other functions as are specified elsewhere in the present Charter or as may be assigned to it by the General Assembly.

198

VOTING

Article 67

1. Each member of the Economic and Social Council shall have one vote.

2. Decisions of the Economic and Social Council shall be made by a majority of the members present and voting.

PROCEDURE

Article 68

The Economic and Social Council shall set up commissions in economic and social fields and for the promotion of human rights, and such other commissions as may be required for the performance of its functions.

Article 69

The Economic and Social Council shall invite any Member of the United Nations to participate, without vote, in its deliberations on any matter of particular concern to that Member.

Article 70

The Economic and Social Council may make arrangements for representatives of the specialized agencies to participate, without vote, in its deliberations and in those of the commissions established by it, and for its representatives to participate in the deliberations of the specialzed agencies.

Article 71

The Economic and Social Council may make suitable arrangements for consultation with non-governmental organizations which are concerned with matters within its competence. Such arrangements may be made with international organizations and, where appropriate, with national organizations after consultation with the Member of the United Nations concerned.

Article 72

1. The Economic and Social Council shall adopt its own rules of procedure, including the method of selecting its President.

2. The Economic and Social Council shall meet as required

in accordance with its rules, which shall include provision for the convening of meetings on the request of a majority of its members.

CHAPTER XI

Declaration Regarding Non-Self-Governing Territories

Article 73

Members of the United Nations which have or assume responsibilities for the administration of territories whose peoples have not yet attained a full measure of self-government recognize the principle that the interests of the inhabitants of these territories are paramount, and accept as a sacred trust the obligation to promote to the utmost, within the system of international peace and security established by the present Charter, the well-being of the inhabitants of these territories, and, to this end:

a. to ensure, with due respect for the culture of the peoples concerned, their political, economic, social, and educational advancement, their just treatment, and their protection against abuses;

b. to develop self-government, to take due account of the political aspirations of the peoples, and to assist them in the progressive development of their free political institutions, according to the particular circumstances of each territory and its peoples and their varying stages of advancement;

c. to further international peace and security;

d. to promote constructive measures of development, to encourage research, and to cooperate with one another and, when and where appropriate, with specialized international bodies with a view to the practical achievement of the social, economic, and scientific purposes set forth in this Article; and

e. to transmit regularly to the Secretary-General for information purposes, subject to such limitation as security and constitutional considerations may require, statistical and other information of a technical nature relating to economic, social, and educational conditions in the territories for which they are respectively responsible other than those territories to which Chapters XII and XIII apply.

Article 74

Members of the United Nations also agree that their policy in respect of the territories to which this Chapter applies, no less than in respect of their metropolitan areas, must be based on the general principle of good-neighborliness, due account being taken of the interests and well-being of the rest of the world, in social, economic, and commercial matters.

CHAPTER XII

International Trusteeship System

Article 75

The United Nations shall establish under its authority an international trusteeship system for the administration and supervision of such territories as may be placed thereunder by subsequent individual agreements. These territories are hereinafter referred to as trust territories.

Article 76

The basic objectives of the trusteeship system, in accordance with the Purposes of the United Nations laid down in Article 1 of the present Charter, shall be:

a. to further international peace and security;

b. to promote the political, economic, social, and educational advancement of the inhabitants of the trust territories, and their progressive development towards self-government or independence as may be appropriate to the particular circumstances of each territory and its peoples and the freely expressed wishes of the peoples concerned, and as may be provided by the terms of each trusteeship agreement;

c. to encourage respect for human rights and for fundamental freedoms for all without distinction as to race, sex, language, or religion, and to encourage recognition of the interdependence of the peoples of the world; and

d. to ensure equal treatment in social, economic, and commercial matters for all Members of the United Nations and their nationals, and also equal treatment for the latter in the administration of justice, without prejudice to the attainment of the foregoing objectives and subject to the provisions of Article 80.

Article 77

1. The trusteeship system shall apply to such territories in the following categories as may be placed thereunder by means of trusteeship agreements:

a. territories now held under mandate;

b. territories which may be detached from enemy states as a result of the Second World War; and

c. territories voluntarily placed under the system by states responsible for their administration.

2. It will be a matter for subsequent agreement as to which territories in the foregoing categories will be brought under the trusteeship system and upon what terms.

Article 78

The trusteeship system shall not apply to territories which have become Members of the United Nations, relationship among which shall be based on respect for the principle of sovereign equality.

Article 79

The terms of trusteeship for each territory to be placed under the trusteeship system, including any alteration or amendment, shall be agreed upon by the states directly concerned, including the mandatory power in the case of territories held under mandate by a Member of the United Nations, and shall be approved as provided for in Articles 83 and 85.

Article 80

1. Except as may be agreed upon in individual trusteeship agreements, made under Articles 77, 79, and 81, placing each territory under the trusteeship system, and until such agreements have been concluded, nothing in this Chapter shall be construed in or of itself to alter in any manner the rights whatsoever of any states or any peoples or the terms of existing international instruments to which Members of the United Nations may respectively be parties.

2. Paragraph 1 of this Article shall not be interpreted as giving grounds for delay or postponement of the negotiation and conclusion of agreements for placing mandated and other territories under the trusteeship system as provided for in Article 77.

Article 81

The trusteeship agreement shall in each case include the terms under which the trust territory will be administered and designate the authority which will exercise the administration of the trust territory. Such authority, hereinafter called the administering authority, may be one or more states or the Organization itself.

There may be designated, in any trusteeship agreement, a strategic area or areas which may include part or all of the trust territory to which the agreement applies, without prejudice to any special agreement or agreements made under Article 43.

1. All functions of the United Nations relating to strategic areas, including the approval of the terms of the trusteeship agreements and of their alteration or amendment, shall be exercised by the Security Council.

2. The basic objectives set forth in Article 76 shall be applicable to the people of each strategic area.

3. The Security Council shall, subject to the provisions of the trusteeship agreements and without prejudice to security considerations, avail itself of the assistance of the Trusteeship Council to perform those functions of the United Nations under the trusteeship system relating to political, economic, social, and educational matters in the strategic areas.

It shall be the duty of the administering authority to ensure that the trust territory shall play its part in the maintenance of international peace and security. To this end the administering authority may make use of volunteer forces, facilities, and assistance from the trust territory in carrying out the obligations towards the Security Council undertaken in this regard by the administering authority, as well as for local defense and the maintenance of law and order within the trust territory.

1. The functions of the United Nations with regard to trusteeship agreements for all areas not designated as strategic, including the approval of the terms of the trusteeship agreements and of their alteration or amendment, shall be exercised by the General Assembly.

2. The Trusteeship Council, operating under the authority

of the General Assembly, shall assist the General Assembly in carrying out these functions.

CHAPTER XIII

The Trusteeship Council

COMPOSITION

Article 86

1. The Trusteeship Council shall consist of the following Members of the United Nations:

a. those Members administering trust territories;

b. such of those Members mentioned by name in Article 23 as are not administering trust territories; and

c. as many other Members elected for three-year terms by the General Assembly as may be necessary to ensure that the total number of members of the Trusteeship Council is equally divided between those Members of the United Nations which administer trust territories and those which do not.

2. Each member of the Trusteeship Council shall designate one specially qualified person to represent it therein.

FUNCTIONS AND POWERS

Article 87

The General Assembly and, under its authority, the Trusteeship Council, in carrying out their functions, may:

a. consider reports submitted by the administering authority;

b. accept petitions and examine them in consultation with the administering authority;

c. provide for periodic visits to the respective trust territories at times agreed upon with the administering authority; and

d. take these and other actions in conformity with the terms of the trusteeship agreements.

Article 88

The Trusteeship Council shall formulate a questionnaire on the political, economic, social, and educational advancement of the inhabitants of each trust territory, and the administering authority for each trust territory within the competence of the

General Assembly shall make an annual report to the General Assembly upon the basis of such questionnaire.

VOTING

Article 89

1. Each member of the Trusteeship Council shall have one vote.

2. Decisions of the Trusteeship Council shall be made by a majority of the members present and voting.

PROCEDURE

Article 90

1. The Trusteeship Council shall adopt its own rules of procedure, including the method of selecting its President.

2. The Trusteeship Council shall meet as required in accordance with its rules, which shall include provision for the convening of meetings on the request of a majority of its members.

Article 91

The Trusteeship Council shall, when appropriate, avail itself of the assistance of the Economic and Social Council and of the specialized agencies in regard to matters with which they are respectively concerned.

CHAPTER XIV

The International Court of Justice

Article 92

The International Court of Justice shall be the principal judicial organ of the United Nations. It shall function in accordance with the annexed Statute, which is based upon the Statute of the Permanent Court of International Justice and forms an integral part of the present Charter.

Article 93

1. All Members of the United Nations are *ipso facto* parties to the Statute of the International Court of Justice.

2. A state which is not a Member of the United Nations may become a party to the Statute of the International Court of Justice on conditions to be determined in each case by the General Assembly upon the recommendation of the Security Council.

1. Each Member of the United Nations undertakes to comply with the decision of the International Court of Justice in any case to which it is a party.

2. If any party to a case fails to perform the obligations incumbent upon it under a judgment rendered by the Court, the other party may have recourse to the Security Council, which may, if it deems necessary, make recommendations or decide upon measures to be taken to give effect to the judgment.

Nothing in the present Charter shall prevent Members of the United Nations from entrusting the solution of their differences to other tribunals by virtue of agreements already in existence or which may be concluded in the future.

1. The General Assembly or the Security Council may request the Interntional Court of Justice to give an advisory opinion on any legal question.

2. Other organs of the United Nations and specialized agencies, which may at any time be so authorized by the General Assembly, may also request advisory opinions of the Court on legal questions arising within the scope of their activities.

CHAPTER XV

The Secretariat

Article 97

The Secretariat shall comprise a Secretary-General and such staff as the Organization may require. The Secretary-General shall be appointed by the General Assembly upon the recommendation of the Security Council. He shall be the chief administrative officer of the Organization.

Article 98

The Secretary-General shall act in that capacity in all meetings of the General Assembly, of the Security Council, of the Economic and Social Council, and of the Trusteeship Council, and shall perform such other functions as are entrusted to him by these organs. The Secretary-General shall make an annual report to the General Assembly on the work of the Organization.

Article 99

The Secretary-General may bring to the attention of the Security Council any matter which in his opinion may threaten the maintenance of international peace and security.

Article 100

1. In the performance of their duties the Secretary-General and the staff shall not seek or receive instructions from any government or from any other authority external to the Ogranization. They shall refrain from any action which might reflect on their position as international officials responsible only to the Organization.

2. Each Member of the United Nations undertakes to respect the exclusively international character of the responsibilities of the Secretary-General and the staff and not to seek to influence them in the discharge of their responsibilities.

Article 101

1. The staff shall be appointed by the Secretary-General under regulations established by the General Assembly.

2. Appropriate staffs shall be permanently assigned to the Economic and Social Council, the Trusteeship Council, and, as required, to other organs of the United Nations. These staffs shall form a part of the Secretariat.

3. The paramount consideration in the employment of the staff and in the determination of the condition of service shall be the necessity of securing the highest standards of efficiency, competence, and integrity. Due regard shall be paid to the importance of recruiting the staff on as wide a geographical basis as possible.

CHAPTER XVI

Miscellaneous Provisions

Article 102

1. Every treaty and every international agreement entered into by any Member of the United Nations after the present Charter comes into force shall as soon as possible be registered with the Secretariat and published by it.

2. No party to any such treaty or international agreement which has not been registered in accordance with the provisions of paragraph 1 of this Article may invoke that treaty or agreement before any organ of the United Nations.

Article 103

In the event of a conflict between the obligations of the Members of the United Nations under the present Charter and their obligations under any other international agreement, their obligations under the present Charter shall prevail.

Article 104

The Organization shall enjoy in the territory of each of its Members such legal capacity as may be necessary for the exercise of its functions and the fulfillment of its purposes.

Article 105

1. The Organization shall enjoy in the territory of each of its Members such privileges and immunities as are necessary for the fulfillment of its purposes.

2. Representatives of the Members of the United Nations and officials of the Organization shall similarly enjoy such privileges and immunities as are necessary for the independent exercise of their functions in connection with the Organidation.

3. The General Assembly may make recommendations with a view to determining the details of the application of paragraphs 1 and 2 of this Article or may propose conventions to the Members of the United Nations for this purpose.

CHAPTER XVII

Transitional Security Arrangements

Article 106

Pending the coming into force of such special agreements referred to in Article 43 as in the opinion of the Security Council enable it to begin the exercise of its responsibilities under Article 42, the parties to the Four-Nation Declaration, signed at Moscow, October 30, 1943, and France, shall, in accordance with the provisions of paragraph 5 of that Declaration, consult with one another and as occasion requires with other Members of the United Nations with a view to such joint action on behalf of the Organization as may be necessary for the purpose of maintaining international peace and security.

Article 107

Nothing in the present Charter shall invalidate or preclude action, in relation to any state which during the Second World War has been an enemy of any signatory to the present Charter, taken or authorized as a result of that war by the Governments having responsibility for such action.

CHAPTER XVIII

Amendments

Article 108

Amendments to the present Charter shall come into force for all Members of the United Nations when they have been adopted by a vote of two thirds of the members of the General Assembly and ratified in accordance with their respective constitutional processes by two thirds of the Members of the United Nations, including all the permanent members of the Security Council.

Article 109

1. A General Conference of the Members of the United Nations for the purpose of reviewing the present Charter may be held at a date and place to be fixed by a two-thirds vote of the General Assembly and by a vote of any seven members of

the Security Council. Each Member of the United Nations shall have one vote in the conference.

2. Any alteration of the present Charter recommended by a two-thirds vote of the conference shall take effect when ratified in accordance with their respective constitutional processes by two thirds of the Members of the United Nations including all the permanent members of the Security Council.

3. If such a conference has not been held before the tenth annual session of the General Assembly following the coming into force of the present Charter, the proposal to call such a conference shall be placed on the agenda of that session of the General Assembly, and the conference shall be held if so decided by a majority vote of the members of the General Assembly and by a vote of any seven members of the Security Council.

CHAPTER XIX

Ratification and Signature

Article 110

1. The present Charter shall be ratified by the signatory states in accordance with their respective constitutional processes.

2. The ratifications shall be deposited with the Government of the United States of America, which shall notify all the signatory states of each deposit as well as the Secretary-General of the Organization when he has been appointed.

3. The present Charter shall come into force upon the deposit of ratifications by the Republic of China, France, the Union of Soviet Socialist Republics, the United Kingdom of Great Britain and Northern Ireland, and the United States of America, and by a majority of the other signatory states. A protocol of the ratifications deposited shall thereupon be drawn up by the Government of the United States of America which shall communicate copies thereof to all the signatory states.

4. The states signatory to the present Charter which ratify it after it has come into force will become original Members of the United Nations on the date of the deposit of their respective ratifications.

Article 111

The present Charter, of which the Chinese, French, Russian, English, and Spanish texts are equally authentic, shall remain deposited in the archives of the Government of the United States of America. Duly certified copies thereof shall be transmitted by that Government to the Governments of the other signatory states.

IN FAITH WHEREOF the representatives of the Governments of the United Nations have signed the present Charter.

DONE at the city of San Francisco the twenty-sixth day of June, one thousand nine hundred and forty-five.